REBELS THAT BREAK THINGS
A BLACK SHEEP MANIFESTO

Find your way. Do your thing.
Have the impact you crave.

BOBBY FORD

LOVE NOTES

Grams, my rock & mentor.
You are missed and loved.

Friends & Partners, you kept me paddling.
I am forever in your debt.

Mark Becker, no greater ally exists.
Many thanks, Friend.

Bridge To Shore, you saved my life and
then taught me how to live it. Much love.

Wicket & Peanut, you are forever
in my heart, my sweet pups.

The Performing Arts, our projects, ignited
my soul. You are my touchstone.

George Lucas, your heroes, kept me in
the fight. Thank you, Master Jedi.

Felicia Day, you wrote one hell of a book.
My weird is loud and proud!

HEARTFELT THANKS

Art Fuentes. Your art brought magic to this rebel tome and elevated its impact. The cast & crew of Hamilton. Your musical genius became the metronome for this book! Easter Eggs in homage abound. Adiana Vega. Thank you for that final bit of polish on the book title. Brio Cooney. Your insights on the first few chapters and your enduring friendship are a blessing beyond words. Book Baby Publishing. Thanks for your stellar support.

DEDICATION

To my fellow Black Sheep, may this book honor
your value and empower your journey. Continue to
change the world one wild idea at a time.

CONTENTS

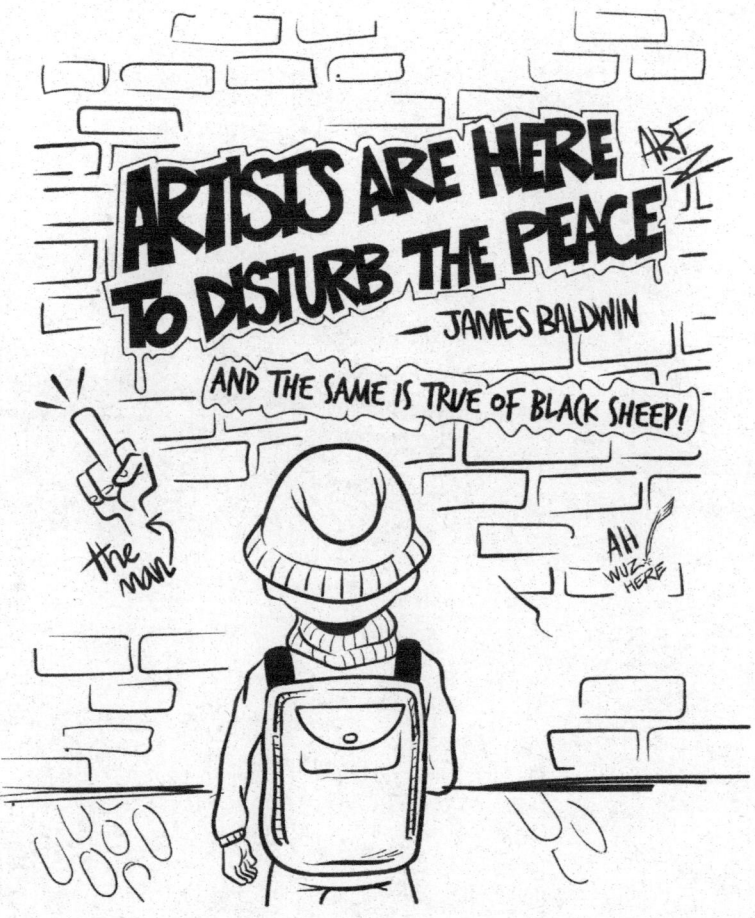

CHAPTER #1
THE NOTE

Photos gathering dust on hard drives. Decades of thank you notes tucked away in a box. Revisiting cherished memories is rarely top of mind. Yet there they are, the memories, the moments, the life I have lived. Twenty photographs went into frames, with several hundred more landing in a photo album. I need those reminders of the story thus far written.

It's easy to forget.

As I wade through cards and images from decades past, I get a glimpse of myself. A warm breeze of sentiment stirs. Chapters of my life, seen in a new light.

In the corporate world, I was the rogue business sage. In the ad game, the visionary brand builder. Shattering the status quo was my modus operandi. University? Not a single class. Business as usual? Hard pass! Vanilla has never been my friend.

On the flip side, I spent fifteen years doing amateur projects in film, improv, and theater. The performing arts set loose my soul! In doing the work, my voice took hold. As is often the case, I found joy outside the lines. Pushing the boundaries in theater or film was liberating. Meaningful. Welcome to the Badlands!

I can be playful as a puppy, then serious as a heart attack. My soul food is people's stories and struggles. Dreams chased. Challenges embraced. I'm generous to a fault but have a visceral edge when cornered.

The Yin with the Yang.
It's always a juggling act.

Dig deeper, and you'll find an aspiring beach bum. Paradise is white sand, ocean breezes, and the rhythmic sounds of crashing waves. Toss in some Bob Marley, and I'm in heaven! No noise. Just life.

My accomplishments, the experiences I hold close, are beyond my wildest childhood dreams. I've also hit rock bottom. It's a gut-wrenching trial. But that's the rodeo. That's the price we pay to get to the good stuff. The moments we put in photo albums, and the thank you notes we tuck away in boxes.

The words etched on the page are born from a lifetime of beating impossible odds. It is knowledge passed down the old-fashioned way, through stories and lessons learned. Pain endured. Tools gathered along the way. I offer these words as a flawed, imperfect being. May they serve you well! Together, we walk.

Ultimately, I wrote the book I needed as a young man, but it did not exist. Once that washed over me, the words began to flow. How to craft a *rogue literary experience* that delivers a lasting impact? To get there, I had to take some risks.

But, who am I to take you on such a journey? To answer that question, we need to do a little time travel.

ESSAY #1: EMANCIPATION

Handsome with a vacant look in his eyes, his Porsche screamed to life. We didn't go anywhere. The stranger and I just sat there, encased in plush leather seats. Loud deafening music purged the need for polite conversation. My mother was prey. I was a means to an end.

One night, an ordinary night, I walked in on this man hovering over my mother's motionless body. She had suffered another booze-infused blackout. A rancid fog of cigarette smoke hung in the air. Something felt off. His malice tore through the nicotine haze. I dragged him off my mother and out the front door. Soon after, cops stood in our living room.

I was fifteen years old.

One of the cops pulled me aside. It was not his first visit to our apartment. We need to talk, he said. If I stayed, the nightmare would never end. Worse, I would suffer the same fate. It was a monumental wake-up call. I sued my parents for emancipation. Your Honor, trust me, they don't meet the job requirements! The State Of California agreed. I was legally an adult by age sixteen.

While my mom survived that night, others like it, the weight of her wounds was no longer mine to carry. The cop taught me an important lesson that night. My power is my own, but that power is worthless unless I use it, no matter the cost.

Claim your power.
Rise without compromise.

ESSAY #2: THE RAINMAKER

Surrounding me was a small group of notable community leaders. The photo shoot, smile-click, was for a magazine article about my consultative work in the region. My client base included the local chapter of a national non-profit, two economic development organizations, a city and county government, and a law firm with thirty-plus partners.

The odds against this level of success were staggering! Hard work and extensive self-study paved the way. When life slammed the door shut, I kicked it open. Failure was never an option.

I learned how to make rain.

The anguish from my childhood became fuel to succeed. Buyer beware! This does not happen overnight. Transforming deep wounds into powerful assets is a lengthy endeavor. Eventually, patiently, street smarts became the hallmark of my brand. By my late thirties, I had been a National Sales Manager, the GM of one ad agency, and the owner of another. By my early fifties, I had been a management consultant for sixteen years and a Creative Director for twenty. I have done paid speaking gigs for groups large and small.

Early in my career, I doubled down on my Black Sheep edge. Had I not done so, you would not be reading this book. A single choice can alter the course of your life.

ESSAY #3: SMUGGLERS BLOOD

Trauma cuts to the marrow. The longer the trauma endures, the deeper the cuts. Unfortunately, my suffering started at birth and lasted twenty-plus years.

Where have the memories of my youth gone? You never shake the loss of your wonder years. Beneath my skin, tattooed on bone, the wounds of old.

Childhood was survival.
Innocence was a weakness.

I had an 85% chance of ending up dead or in jail by age thirty. That was the *expert opinion* of one therapist. Another predicted a life spent picking up the pieces. I was a broken toy with little hope of repair. The odds are not in your favor! The experts' felt I deserved the truth. As the great philosopher Han Solo once said, "Never tell me the odds!" I guess I have smuggler's blood in my veins. The experts were dead wrong.

Titles do not equal expertise.
Advice does not equal wisdom.

Why are you so outspoken? You have opinions on everything! Why can't you be more pragmatic? You take too many risks! The message was clear.

Know your place.
Shut your mouth.
Go with the flow.

Yeah, that's not going to happen. Obedient and silent is not how I roll. I'm the racehorse that always beats the odds. The Fire Within refuses to settle for anything less. The Japanese have a word for that fire, Kuyashii, using the doubt of others as motivation to succeed. Chef Niki Nakayama spoke of it on the Netflix show, Chef's Table.

When the status quo tries to silence my voice, I speak louder. When naysayers try to bring me in line, I cross the line. When the world seems impossible, I blaze a trail. When it all gets to be too much, I binge ice cream. To beat the odds, harness The Fire Within.

ESSAY #4: MR. DIRECTOR

All I do is work! Perhaps a crash course on Filmmaking? There's no business like show business! Why not? It sounds fun. A single act of whimsy let loose my artistic soul. In many ways, it was the first time I felt truly alive.

I was forty-three years old.

The process of telling stories with pictures kidnapped every ounce of my being. Over several years, I attended numerous filmmaking intensives in Los Angeles and Austin. Books on cinematic storytelling were consumed with reckless abandon. I attended the Austin Film

Festival several years in a row. Finally! People that got me. We spoke a common language.

Filmmaking was art therapy. My work was brief, six years, two short films, one of them premiering in the UK. At best, I dabbled. And yet, the filmmaking process ignited my imagination on a whole new level. Seeing my work on the big screen, followed by a tour through film festivals, was thrilling. It was beyond my comprehension.

What about acting? I could never memorize the lines! Maybe improv? Bingo! Two improv schools and countless intensives later, I was hooked. There are no words for the power of improv. It's a therapeutic roller coaster with a side of Sesame Street.

Can Bobby come out and play?
I finally got to be a kid!

A classmate and I put together an improv duo that did over thirty shows in New York City accents. How is that even possible? The magic of telling improvised stories on tiny stages to tiny audiences is exhilarating. It got me thinking. How to unleash the dramatic potential of improv in a black box theater?

The answer came from an improv show where a young gay man, a member of the audience, bravely shared the shame he felt coming out. His truth was so piercing that it stuck with me. I decided to transform several of Samuel Beckett's one-act plays into a theatrical improv format. To do so was heresy. I called the show Breaking Beckett.

I had no training in directing theater. How the hell was I going to pull this off? I had to age myself twenty years using theatrical makeup! Are you fracking kidding me? Would anyone show up? I was flying without a net. The format was intense, absurd, dramatic, and entirely improvised to include the music. The cast and crew were a gift without equal.

Each show ended with the cast lowering their heads and shuffling, as a group, downstage towards the audience. Once settled, the protagonist, which changed each show, slowly raised their head to deliver one of my favorite Beckett lines.

"I pause to record that I feel in extraordinary form. Delirium perhaps."

Beloved Austin writer Wayne Allan Brenner described the show as "psychotherapy as a team spectator sport." Frank Benge wrote, "One of the main functions of theatre is to make an audience think. In this regard, Breaking Beckett, now playing at The Institution Theater, succeeds. I will probably be thinking about this piece for some time to come." Entertaining people has never been my thing. Getting people to think? Pure adrenaline! The reviews hit home. My True North was changing course. It was hard to process.

All of my experiences in film, theater, and improv trace back to a single decision to trust my curiosity. Who knew it would have such an impact? The performing arts broke through decades of emotional concrete. We can't predict the game changers, but we can follow the heat. Life is in the here and now. Jump off the cliff!

BLACK SHEEP PROUD™

The pressure to fit in is enormous. Everywhere we turn, one message churns. Being different is bad. Go with the flow. Protect the status quo. Odd is the duck that rejects those archaic norms. But for Black Sheep, reject them we must. We don't have a choice. It's in our DNA.

Black Sheep entrepreneurs forcefully dismiss business as usual. Extraordinary happens when an obsession takes control! How to nurture ground-breaking ideas that could alter an entire industry? Step one, toss out the rule book! Disruption breaks things to unlock their true potential. Companies like Patagonia, Tom's Shoes, Fast Company, and Pixar come to mind.

Any business can push the envelope. Any owner can radically redefine their space. It has nothing to do with the size of your company. It has everything to do with the fire in your heart.

Build the game changer!

Black Sheep creators see the world through a different pair of glasses. Inquisitive by nature, they explore as young children play. When a project captures their imagination, they make it happen. Black Sheep Creators chart their own course. Felicia Day's geek empire, Lin Manuel Miranda's musical Hamilton, and Lisa Ling's visionary work as a television journalist come to mind.

The trait these prolific creators have in common is their signature work. It stands alone. You know when you're in the presence of their craft. I remember going to Hyde Park Theater here in Austin, Texas. The theater seats maybe a hundred people. They were putting on a throwback USO holiday show with a tiny cast. It remains one of the best black box productions I've ever seen!

I'm not encouraging you to chase a grandiose version of artistic success. I'm encouraging you to do the art you love! What type of projects ignites your need to create? What would you produce if there were no rules? Take risks. Be vulnerable. Get seen.

Do the work that feeds your soul.

Black Sheep disruptors are truth-tellers who rattle cages for a living. Unapologetic and opinionated, these folks blow up the status quo. In keeping it real, they hold us to a higher standard. If you don't like rocking the boat, this path is not for you! Dr. Jason Johnson, Gary Vaynerchuk, and Glennon Doyle come to mind.

My kind of people! Yet, very different people, one to the next. Black Sheep truth-tellers defy labels. They stand their ground, even when doing so raises the temperature. Although plenty try, you can't fake that level of audacity or expertise. The gospel they preach is born from real-world experience. It's wisdom that was earned the hard way. The words they speak break through the noise.

Truth tellers don't whisper.

Black Sheep activists take on the issues that plague humankind. When the world aches, they get to work.

When all hope is lost, they light the way. Big things need to happen! It's trench warfare of the visionary kind. Stacey Abrams, Beto O'Rourke, GISH, and Moms Demand Action come to mind.

But who am I to change the world? The timing isn't right. I'm not ready! As my friend, Dr. Karim Currey, once said, "Every revolutionary had to pick up a cross." Have you picked up your cross? Champions of change are not born. They grow into the role over time.

Turn your outrage into action.

I have mentioned but a few types of Black Sheep. Our kind does not easily fit into categories or labels. Nowhere does this truth become more apparent than when I try to write my social media bio. It's a special type of hell! Yes, I am a writer. The artisan craft of putting words on the page matters to me, but the words serve a much broader purpose. So, am I a writer? The same can be said of my work as a director, producer, improviser, teacher, creator, progressive, marketer, and such. So, what do I put on my fracking social media bio?

Black Sheep ignore the status quo. Our path is our own. We think for ourselves because we respect the *sovereignty* of our minds.

Being different is a beauty mark.
Wear it with pride!

Few people champion Black Sheep as soulfully as Lori Deschene, founder of the blog Tiny Buddha. Her content feels like a warm hug from a beloved friend. One of her social media posts, titled *"I love weirdos"* by Creig Crippen, holds a special place in my heart. Whenever I needed to bond with my audience for this book, that quote, the stunning artwork, instantly connected me with my Black Sheep tribe.

Take pride in your path.
Anchor your journey.

Many types of people will find treasure in this offbeat manifesto. Some identify as Black Sheep, while others do not. That's ok! Independent thinking and creating will free you from the dark abyss known as autopilot. Get curious. Take a few risks. Who knows? You might surprise yourself! Open new doors. Explore uncharted territory.

I have been a thorn in polite society's ass for decades. I'm a different kind of dude! At first, I felt like an outcast. What is wrong with me? Then, I tried to fit in. You know, do life *the proper way.* That didn't work! Thankfully, I broke free from the obligation to be someone other than myself. Listen to your discontent! Add fuel to the fire. The remedy for suffocation is fresh air.

Despite the trauma, impossible odds, the so-called experts, and the people who lacked imagination, I rose from the ashes. Society did not see nor encourage my potential, yet, there it was, hard at work. The idea that success requires fitting into a box that never rocks is bullshit. Blow up the box!

Being Black Sheep Proud™ has nothing to do with bravado, buzz words, narcissism, or justifying toxic behavior. As a movement, we are the polar opposite of those traits. We embrace candor, chart our own course, and do the bold thing because those actions align with who we are as human beings. Black Sheep Proud™ is not a phrase that seeks superficial praise. It's the real deal. Take pride in your independence.

High atop the pedestal where heroes live is an empty space. We walk together as equals. All that I have to offer is my experience, strength and hope. It's a concept from my 12 Step days. Central to my story is trauma and how I used it as a fire to succeed. Your life experience is your own. Black Sheep come from every walk of life, each with their own story to tell. Everyone has dreams to build, demons to slay, and obstacles to overcome. Our journey is shared. That is our common ground.

WEATHER THE STORM

Amanda Gorman shared a story on Instagram about her stunning inaugural poem, *"The Hill We Climb."* I replied, "How to wake up a nation that refuses to feel?" Therein is the dilemma. How to awaken your mystical might if you avoid the inner work that sets it free? The hunger to do more than survive requires sturdy legs. Willpower alone is not enough. Resilience is the elixir that wins the race. It's the key that opens the door to hope. Options. Untapped potential.

What to do when the storms of life are too much to bear? How to stay the course? Over the years, filled with fears, many talented souls have left their dreams behind. It's impossible to conceive. Evolving into the life you crave. A bold vision made real. Peace of mind. There's no place to hide when everything is on the line. Will you sink or swim? Will you dig deeper than you ever thought possible? A house is as strong as its foundation. Please, do the internal work covered in the next three chapters. Unlock the kind of fortitude that can weather any storm!

CHAPTER #2

EMBRACE THE STRUGGLE

"Turn your wounds into wisdom"

Oprah Winfrey

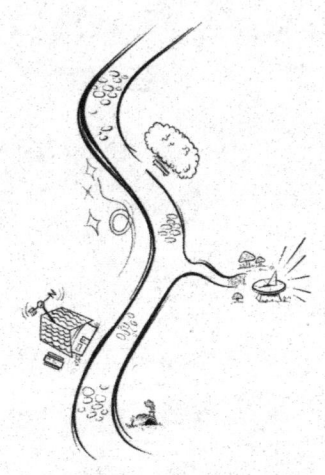

To live is to suffer. Unbearable pain crushes our will to do more than survive. The strain can paralyze the best of us. How to grab our breath when life knocks us down? How to find relief from the grief? Sharing our story creates community. Asking for help lightens the load. Less bravado. More surrender.

The problem is not the struggle itself but our response to the struggle. A lot rides on how we react to the many challenges of life. It's a critical concept for Black Sheep because we take more risks. With risk comes suffering. How to stay the course? To steady our resolve, we must embrace our humanity. Think less. Feel more.

The trials of life either give you an excuse to stay stuck or kindling to thrive, to be fully alive, no matter the odds. Will you feed the darkness, or will you feed the light? When standing at a crossroads, you have to pick a path. Which path will you choose?

The challenges of the moment do not determine your fate. Fight for the things you have yet to discover. More will be revealed. Choose to believe in things conceived, born of your heart and mind! The way forward is not always clear, but it's there, waiting for your footsteps.

PERSONAL STRUGGLES

In the final moments of life, what do people regret? It's not popularity, success, wealth, or fame. Guess what self-help books tend to focus on? The four things people don't regret! Are we betting on the wrong horse?

Our emotions, especially intense ones, are a problem. That's what we're taught. Walk away! To embrace the struggle is to embrace the feelings that come with that struggle. Autopilot keeps us stuck. It's how we disappear from the world, even from ourselves. Weathering the storm is hard, and yet, weather the storm we must. It helps to know other people struggle with the same challenges. We're not alone.

ESSAY #1: BROKENNESS

Transitioning from my traumatic past into adulthood was brutal. Daily life was a constant tidal wave of anxiety. The world felt dangerous. I remember going on a blind date with a ravishing girl during my early twenties. Mid-date, I melted down. What was I thinking? Panic set in like a plague. When a friend picked me up, I was visibly trembling, flooded by the complexities of adulting.

The shame was immense.
What is wrong with me?

My solution was bartending school, followed by working at a high-volume bar. How's everyone doing tonight? Cue the smolder! Shots, anyone? I was teaching myself to swim in the deep end without realizing that was happening. A decade later, I was doing paid speaking gigs.

The road from mid-date meltdown to public speaking was not a straight one. There was much to learn with plenty of setbacks. Trust me, it was harsh. But I did learn and eventually found my footing. Finding our way is an awkward undertaking. I'm drowning in embarrassment! It's great to be alive! Such is the journey. How else to come into our own?

While severe anxiety may not be something you battle, the whole point of this section is clear. Go to bartending school! Ok, so that's totally not the point. Everybody is broken to varying degrees. We all fight internal battles. Human beings are messy, and imperfection has no cure.

The things we face, we embrace.
The things we ignore, we store.
Empty the shelves.

Not long ago, I was watching Oprah in a series she did on mental health. There was this tender moment when her voice changed from Oprah, the media mogul, to Oprah, the young traumatized girl. Tears welled up, and her voice cracked. Trauma survivors know Oprah's tears all too well. We have shed the same tears. The least we can do is give them a voice.

Expressing sorrow empowers us.
Hiding sorrow enslaves us.

Are you starting to see a pattern? When stuck in a closet, kick down the door! Fair warning, there's lots of door kicking in this tome. The blades that once cut you do not define you. At some point, you need to claim your power or the potential of tomorrow never happens. When the wounds run deep, that can feel unachievable. Walk with purpose. Persist with passion.

Numbing out. Overcompensating. Neither makes for good medicine. Why hide? Why lie? Why deny your truth? Be you, fully revealed. Here the frack I am, world! Buckle up! Transparency is empowering. Reach for the stars while dancing with your demons. It's a two-step we all must learn. Messy is its own kind of beautiful.

ESSAY #2: NOISE

HBO Max put out a six-part series called 100 Foot Wave. It stirred up memories of my teenage youth. I remember sitting on my surfboard, the sun coming up or down, spotting wave sets. I loved that aspect of surfing. It felt spiritual. In the name of full disclosure, I was a horrible surfer! My one consolation prize is the scar on my big toe from a nasty wipeout. Bragging rights, Yo!

Sitting on the back of the Pacific Ocean, the world felt much bigger than my childhood woes. The swell of Mother Nature rising and falling, and me, this tiny spec, along for the ride. I was Her guest. That was always clear. It was comforting. Soothing.

Serenity gets lost in the noise.
Remove the noise.

In watching the HBO special, I realized the lesson. My wetsuit, surfboard, and surfing technique (which did not exist) were of no consequence. Are you here with me, Bobby Ford? Are you fully present? Those were the questions Mother Nature posed as I floated on Her spine or surrendered to the might of Her whitewash. Life, with its many challenges, requires us to show up.

Writing about struggle makes me think about Anthony Bourdain. I suspect he had a hard time removing the noise. Eventually, it became too much. I don't judge Tony for taking his own life, but I miss his edgy presence. He always had a way of humanizing our world. On so many levels, Tony was unapologetically Black Sheep. To walk our path exacts a toll. In my view, it's a grind worth enduring. But when is the price too high? What to do when the darkness never fades?

You are more than a label.
There is nothing to prove.
Raise the white flag.

Up through my late thirties, daily life felt like an endless tornado, with me spinning about in the eye of the storm. I loved the thrill. I hated the price tag. What's the meaning of life? More fun! More sex! It's three in the morning. Let's drive to Las Vegas! Why not? Ain't life grand. Ah, yes, the barnstorming days of my impulsive youth. Whenever I crashed from skiing tornados, recovery groups helped me pick up the pieces.

While 12 Step fellowships have their flaws (like anything in life), I have yet to experience a more pure form of love. Hugs are plentiful. Feelings are shared without edits, often with a strong dose of humor. Judgment rarely gets in the way. Interestingly, recovery asks the same core questions as Mother Nature. Are you here with me, Bobby Ford? Are you fully present?

Less bullshit.
More truth.
Remove the noise.

In surrender, we find our limits. Our willpower can only take us so far. It's a tough pill to swallow for Black Sheep. We rather like the highs that come from blasting our way through the cosmos! Or, in some cases, the safety of silence. Numbing out. Being invisible. Are you drowning? Is it time to wave the white flag? If so, please, ask for help.

ESSAY #3: ARMOR

After the terrorist attacks on September 11, 2001, the church I belonged to long ago held a twelve-hour prayer vigil. When I showed up, people were hurting. While religious speak was all the rage, meaningful comfort was in short supply. Even when people sobbed, the response was a warm version of sterile at best.

When we refuse to feel, we broker a deal to remain silent. Anything you say can and will be used against you!

Be strong. Move along. Stuff everything inside. Wear thick armor. The feelings will subside. Authentic emotion? Off-limits! Superficial pretense is yummy, like warm apple pie.

> *Oh, hell no!*
> *Never be ashamed of your tears.*
> *You earned them.*

Apologizing for your struggles is apologizing for being a human being. My bad! I'm sorry for taking up space! Your struggles, all the gooey, icky emotions that spill out, verify the *sacred nature* of your existence. The tricky part is not letting those emotions run amok. Have you ever driven when angry? It's a lovely day for a car crash! Let's avoid that scenario.

Assignment #1 / In DBT, a hybrid of Buddhism and cognitive therapy, they teach a skill called Wise Mind. It's a worthy addition to your toolkit. Google the term "Wise Mind Worksheet." Find a version you like, and print a few copies. What has been royally kicking your butt as of late? Write a brief paragraph about the issue. You don't need anything fancy, just enough to clarify the struggle. Once you have your paragraph in hand, work the challenge through the Wise Mind Worksheet, which should include Emotional Mind, Reasonable Mind, and Wise Mind sections. When done, return to this chapter.

What stood out from the worksheet? Jot down anything that comes to mind. Here's the problem. We're hauling ass through life so fast we don't notice all the wreckage along the way! Our capacity to solve problems is immense when we slow down long enough to do the work that elevates our effectiveness.

Reduce the need for speed.
Find the middle ground.

Honestly, there's nothing like a proper ugly cry. Snot flying everywhere. People ducking for cover. Intensely expressing our emotions can be cathartic. Is it wise to make big decisions during such meltdowns? Probably, not. The Wise Mind Worksheet provides clarity.

Hungry for more DBT? Find a therapist that specializes in Dialectical Behavior Therapy in your area. The name is over the top, but the program is a game changer.

PROFESSIONAL STRUGGLES

Hopes and dreams, things imagined in your head, such things you have seen. These ideas of yours *must* be given life! Your art, food, revolution, or radical solution must succeed. The struggle is real. And yet, many have made the journey. Fight for the things you seek to build or create. Life is short. Do your thing.

To push the envelope is to tempt the hands of fate. What if we're kidding ourselves? What if the end result is a stinky pile of garbage? A sane person would walk away! Why go through the stress? While valid emotions, Black Sheep rarely calculate the personal cost. The heart wants what the heart wants. Screw the odds! It's a mentality hardwired into our DNA once we have learned to trust ourselves.

ESSAY#1: WHITE SPACE

Imagine a page, clay, sketch pad, staff paper, whiteboard, recipe book, whatever, that is totally blank. Staring back at you is nothingness, a few ideas, no rules, and no safety net. It's the 100 Foot Wave! Before the founders of Cirque du Soleil brought it to the masses, it did not exist. Before Neil Gaiman brought his edgy worlds to life, they did not exist. Before Ben & Jerry's brought socially conscious ice cream to the masses, it did not exist. Can you imagine life without Cherry Garcia?

Initially, you fail more than you succeed. Pixar started as a software company. It took time for them to become the celebrated animation studio they are today. Why wait? Start failing! Get better at your thing.

Failure is wisdom.
Learn the lessons.

I need to write a book, but the traditional process feels like wandering a fiery desert without a drop of water. How to craft a rebel tome that has an impact? Step one, lock down the book title and cover design. Step two, clarify the key elements of the experience I want to facilitate. Step three, flesh out the artwork that will drive the reader's journey. Step four, lock down nine (now eight) chapter titles. At this point, traditional publishers are popping anxiety meds like they're Skittles! Could I be more of an amateur? Perhaps. Will it take off? I have no idea, but I stand behind my work.

Honor your instincts.
Trust your process.

The book you hold in your hands is, for the most part, as originally conceived. A few changes were made, but the core vision remains intact. Are you giving birth to something that *rises above the crowd*, or are you falling in line? Captain Reynolds said it best, "I aim to misbehave." Do the thing that feeds your fire. If you have to make a mess of things, have at it! Make messes that fill you with pride. That is an essential part of the process.

See that bloody mess over there in the corner? Yep, all me! At first, it pissed everybody off. Now it's kicking ass and taking names. Isn't it lovely? My mind heard a cockney accent when writing this paragraph. That's odd.
If your big idea was born from a blank page, it's a different kind of rodeo. You're doubling down on something that has yet to exist! Personally, I live for those projects. Exploring uncharted territory is a rush, but I'm not going to lie. It's not for the faint of heart. Do you believe in your wild idea? That's the million-dollar question. What say you? Too much or all in?

To be clear, I do not recommend flying solo. Outside counsel and collaboration are essential to the creative process. Effective trailblazing does not happen in a vacuum. At the same, stay true to your vision. Protect the magic you are trying to bring to life.

ESSAY#2: LA VIE BOHÈME

Now more than ever, we need wildlings! Who better to change the world than the rebels setting fire to outdated norms? Light the torch! Granted, there are many types of bohemians. Equal to the number of stars in the sky. Ok, that was nauseating. Still, there is no such thing as a legit bohemian! We come in many flavors with countless points of view. The stereotypes of the 1950s are dated. Breaking the rules, thankfully, remains a thing.

The wildlings of today are reinventing political activism, community building, content distribution, mental health treatment, entertainment, food service and many other areas central to our lives. Modern-day bohemians are redefining how things get done! It's an exciting time to be alive. Twitch/Discord combo communities averaged one hundred million active users each month in 2022. Let that math sink in for more than a minute! The list of Black Sheep products, services, and art you can experience is endless. And they have a few traits in common.

Convention, hard pass.
Free expression, pour another round.
La vie Bohéme!

Double down on your edge. That was the sage advice of Laurence McCahill and Dr. Carlos Saba, founders of The Happy Startup School. Go on then, stir up some trouble! Paint outside the lines! It felt good to be seen. We all need permission in one way or another. I joined their bohemian community during a tough white space era of my life. Lost, burnt out, I was looking for answers.

How to best describe The Happy Startup experience? If Burning Man, Brené Brown, Bob Dylan, and Richard Branson had a baby, and that baby gave you homework, it would be close. Essentially, that's their Brit brilliance in a nutshell. The canvas is blank! Make it your own. Rules? What rules? The seeds I planted under their guidance continue to flourish. But it was their message that spoke to me on a profound level.

Don't grow up.
More imagination, not less.
La vie Bohéme!

How to cope as an empath? How to belong when you live outside of convention? How to not lose yourself as a solo artist? Wildings run best when running in packs. Find your tribe. Connect with your cause. Run wild without pause. Hold nothing back. Let your bohemian star shine.

Find some prime real estate in The Badlands. Make it your own.

ESSAY #3: GO ROGUE

Heavy snow coated the plane as I settled into my seat. It had been a long, intense week. I was troubleshooting a project between a city and an adjacent county. Tears welled up. When the project ended, I walked away from my management consulting practice of sixteen years.

Going rogue fits like a glove. But calling it quits? That was new. I don't quit. Yet, it was time. I knew this without a doubt. Perhaps my career would have gone down a more artistic path in another life? Nothing can be done about that now, but I can do more edgy work in the performing arts. That's where my bliss lives. When we're willing to explore virgin territory, anything can happen.

Where do you need to wander?

Doctors, lawyers, owners, and many others are cashing out to kick off new adventures. The traps most insane are the ones we maintain. Replace mindless with purposeful. Replace obligation with passion. It's never too late to go rogue. Jump in the water. Swim upstream.

If you're done, you know it.
Start the next chapter.

As an aside, all this Black Sheep stuff gets easier with practice. Take a leap of faith. Who knows how it might turn out? Explore your options. Ask tough questions. We discover new possibilities by opening new doors. Begin opening doors!

EXCUSES OR KINDLING

Life, for all its beauty and wonder, is a struggle. How we react to those struggles determines everything. The trials of life either give you an excuse to stay stuck or kindling to thrive, to be fully alive, no matter the odds.

The struggles I highlighted were a mere glimpse of the things that tend to get in the way. Childhood trauma plays a pivotal role in my narrative. Your tale is your own, as are the battles you face. It all gets a bit wonky, doesn't it? Life. Work. Relationships. I've never been all that fond of the phrase "live your best life" because it sells a cliche. A Hollywood version of existence that does not allow for the spectacular yet flawed realities of human behavior.

The most consequential chapter in this book is the one we're navigating. Working through our wounds is easy to avoid. Nope! Not my jam! Everything we dodge leaves an emotional artifact. The things we ignore, we store. Dealing with our shit is rough. At times, it seems impossible. No matter, stick with the work. It's vital work.

When contrasting the trauma of my youth against this book, I'm brought to tears. It's been a long ride. On paper, folks said I didn't stand a chance. What to do? How to respond? Burn the damn paper! Screw the predictions! We are what we choose to become in this life.

MINDFUL PONDERING

Dale Carnegie's *"How To Win Friends And Influence People"* still has me over-tipping waiters and heaping on the praise. I first read the book early in my early twenties. It was published in 1937, over eighty years ago! How did he do it? Mr. Carnegie tapped into a timeless principle regarding human behavior.

Insight lights the torch.
Habits feed the flame.

Tucked away in this Black Sheep Manifesto are six contemplative journaling assignments around six life choices and twelve habits. Each is a seed in search of soil.

Is your mind nutrient-rich? Finding your groove is sacred work. When writing is a reverent act, the words etched on the page have depth and meaning.

Your writing sessions should be free of interruptions, distractions, and anything that takes you astray. Focused, thoughtful writing reveals the answers you seek. Write from a *reverent place of peace.* Honor the importance of your Black Sheep work. Without stakes, nothing shakes, and everything remains the same! Actionable insights paired with tangible tools break new ground.

> *Reading words plants seeds.*
> *Contemplative journaling grows trees.*

What sounds, smells, tastes, and visuals put you into a contemplative state of peak self-awareness? Give it some thought. Create a list. As an aside, different topics require different moods. Create a menu! Handcraft a variety of environments that you can sink into depending upon your needs at the time. Hitting the pause button to reflect and ponder plays a big role in our work together.

CONTEMPLATIVE JOURNALING
Embrace The Struggle

A lot rides on how we react to the many challenges of life. Will you feed the darkness, or will you feed the light? The challenges of the moment do not determine your fate. Fight for the things you have yet to discover.

1) Create a title page. Write Life Choice #1, and then on the next line, write, Embrace The Struggle. Dress up the page with graphics if that's your thing. Make this contemplative session your own!

2) Add a few pages of actionable insights from this chapter. An insight is actionable when it moves you to act in a specific way. If I were reading versus writing this book, I would ask myself, "How can I better embrace the struggle?" Look for insights that inspire you to act!

HABIT #1: LIVE IN THE TRUTH

Living in the truth keeps you on solid, sober ground. Face the facts. Meet the moment. You have what it takes to deal with the situation at hand. Where to begin? Here are a few ideas to get you started.

Wake-Up Calls / Suddenly being called to account is potent. It brings us to our senses. Better to embrace such moments than fight the truths they reveal. What have you been avoiding? How to make the most of these moments when they appear?

Open your eyes.
What do you see?

Acceptance / It is hard to accept the pain that hits bone deep. It's a delicate balancing act between processing your emotions and moving on to heal. What do you need to feel? What do you need to accept? Where are you stuck? Begin the journey of soulful acceptance.

Holding on hurts.
Letting go heals.

Ownership / We all make mistakes, some with lifelong consequences. We all face crossroads we rather avoid. Ownership reclaims our power. What mistakes do you need to own? What situations can no longer be avoided? Ownership plus action closes the deal on progress.

Avoidance feeds the problem.
Ownership starves the problem.

3) Set aside twenty pages to work on the first habit. Use the first page of this habit as the title page. Write, "Embrace The Struggle: Habit #1 - Live In The Truth." Add graphics if that's your thing.

4) How can you get better at living in the truth in an empowering way that is not shaming? What resources do you need? What action steps need to happen? Make it real. Be specific. Develop a new habit. As a reminder,

Rome was not built in a day. Be gentle with yourself! Progress, not perfection.

HABIT #2: LIVE IN THE SOLUTION

Living in the solution unleashes the full might of your talents and resolve. Obstacles are overcome. Demons are slain. Where to begin? Here are a few ideas to get you started.

Find Your Focus / Solving a problem, especially a complex one, requires clarifying your priorities. What is weighing heavy on your mind? Identify the three tasks that will turn the tide.

Prioritize your time.
Clarity is power!

Get Motivated / Big roadblocks. Emotionally charged challenges. Why take them on? What's in it for you? How will you measure success? You are more likely to meet the moment when fired up and ready to rock.

Act with purpose.
Persist with passion.

Do The Work / Turn adversity into an advantage. What have you been putting off? What needs to get done? Plan your work, then work your plan. It's a concept that's been around for decades because it works.

Fight for your dreams.
Settle for nothing less.

5) Set aside twenty pages to work on the second habit. Use the first page of this habit as the title page. Write, "Embrace The Struggle: Habit #2 - Live In The Solution." Add graphics and visuals if that's your thing.

6) How can you get better at living in solution? What resources do you need? What action steps need to happen? Make it real. Be specific. Develop a new habit. As a reminder, Rome was not built in a day.

7) Celebrate! It's not easy to do this kind of work, but it is worthwhile. You are investing in yourself! You are learning to own your Black Sheep voice and powers. Do something nice for yourself. Get in the habit of celebrating your victories, large and small.

Choose to believe in things conceived, born of your heart and mind! The way forward is not always clear, but it's there, waiting for your footsteps.

Embrace the struggle!

CHAPTER #3

HONOR YOUR HUMANITY

"Embrace the glorious mess that you are."

Elizabeth Gilbert

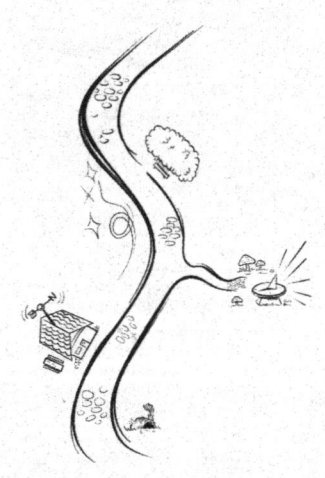

As we heal, we grow. As we realize, we change course. The less we need to prove, the more we accomplish. Self-acceptance is found in the stunning beauty of imperfection. Human complexity is a work of art! Make peace with the person in the mirror.

Loud or quiet, kinky or vanilla, boring or bold, hot or cold, there is no correct way to be a human being! We come in every shape and size, some wild, some wise, just doing our thing. We fall on our faces then soar, thus the endless contradictions that make life worth living.

The hard questions of existence are often the most rewarding to explore. What is the meaning of life? What was I born to do? Does any of it matter? Do I matter? When the answers come easy, the payoff is minimal.

You are enough, just as you are without the upgrades. Nothing you buy makes you more, and nothing you lack makes you less. If the cup is never satisfied, nothing fills the cup. Choose a cup that stays full!

At times I'm weak because it's hard to be strong. Then I feel ok. Catch my stride, followed by a loud crash. Rinse, and repeat. A taste of joy with a bit of strife. Here is what I've come to realize. We could all use a little more grace, some room, some space, as we find our way. Self-acceptance requires progress, not perfection. Wins and losses. Highs and lows. As we dance, we learn.

Dance more.
Think less.

How to accept yourself as you are with no pre-conditions, escape clauses, or awkward pauses when someone compliments you from the heart? You are legit, even if you could be more. There is always more, but for today, you're doing just fine. Your humanity is enough.

THE BATTLE WITHIN

No matter your talent, it will be hard to do your thing if your baggage is the boss. Power, money, nor fame will dull the doubt or ease the pain. Isolation, making yourself small, yet more of the same. This is not to say that all Black Sheep manifest their struggles similarly. Nor is it to say that all forms of acting out are ruinous. Where is the line in the sand?

Surf your rough edges.
Find your sane.

Behind door number one is a tortured soul. To do your thing is to suffer. Behind door number two is a rebel that stands on solid ground. To do your thing is to thrive despite the challenges of life. When tortured, no amount of talent, income, or prestige fills the void. When standing on solid ground, your flaws, the wounds of life, inform, even elevate your work or craft. Which door will you choose?

AM I WORTHY?

The life I've lived and the things I have seen. Normal is not a language I speak. How to feel? How to deal? The broken glass within stands out in a crowd. It's the wrong kind of loud! The skeletons of my past go clackity-clack.

My wounds and regrets hide in a cellar of shame. I welded the door shut, yet the voices remained. How do I quiet the skeletons? How to live a meaningful life as a fallible being? The need to heal and forgive is universal. Nowhere is that more essential than the need to heal and forgive ourselves. Am I a worthy human being? It's a terrifying question. Let's talk about sex.

I know, right?
No warning!

The highs from sex, or more accurately, intense orgasms, can chemically mimic the highs of heroin. Why wouldn't I try to fuck my way to never-ending confidence and bliss? Right? It's like getting stuck at adult Disneyland. In reality, it doesn't work. Not over the long haul. Some of my adventures were fun. No regrets. But it stopped being fun long before I woke up, and the price was steep. I never got to be a dad. That's not easy to write. It's even harder to feel and confess. Worse, I had no idea that I wanted to have children. The downside of being numb at ninety miles per hour. Life in the fast lane.

Sex is just sex. To be clear, I remain a huge fan! It's hot. It's not. It is what it is in the moment. Still, sex doesn't solve life's problems. When we come down from the orgasmic highs, there we are, birthday suit naked. It's hard to be *truly naked* with another human being. This is even more, the case when it comes to the person in the mirror. We all have wounds and regrets. Whether we admit that truth is another story altogether.

Clean out the cellar.
Heal the shame.

How to feel worthy despite our mistakes and flaws? When we refuse to see our frailty from a place of empathy, our sense of worth collapses. We get lost, tormented, not whole, and out of control. We search for peace in places it does not exist.

ESSAY #1: SHARE YOUR STORY

Your accomplishments and talents are worthy of praise, but I'm not talking about that kind of story. Earlier I wrote that all I can do is share my experience, strength, and hope. The same is true of you. Healing happens when you drop the armor.

Telling your story is speaking your truth. Transparency and rigorous honesty are the building blocks for this kind of narrative. Who are you? Tell us about your pain, mistakes made, and the bridges you have burned. What do you regret? What have you learned? It's all there, waiting to be told. Be brave. Be you. Fully revealed, heard, and seen. When people get a taste of your unvarnished truth and say, I get it. I get you. It's ok! Welcome home! No longer alone, the pain and shame are out of the closet. A new day has arrived.

Penny, for your thoughts?
We hide at our own peril.

The flawless execution of a life well lived does not exist. The depth of our wounds, nor the size of our regrets, determine our fate. The damage happens when we ignore the hurt and guilt that goes bump in the night. How to live your best Black Sheep life in silence?

To silence a human voice, any human voice is to dehumanize that individual or group. Why, then, is it ok to silence ourselves? To deny our wounds and mistakes is to deny our humanity. That's not ok! Your brokenness, insights gained, talents that rose, and the dark moments you survived are part of your life. People need your story! Your words will help them as much as they heal you. That's how it works.

Come out of the closet.
Speak your truth.

I have shared the gritty details of my story many times over the years. It's never easy, but it's always important. I remember baring my soul to a group of about fifty, tears pouring down my cheeks the entire time. The applause that resulted had nothing to do with my speaking skills. Everyone in the audience had their own stories of struggle. It just happened to be the week I told mine. To find *community* in our pain is to heal the pain.

The act of confession is sacred. It is a cleansing of the soul. To be clear, I'm not talking about religious confession, although people find that helpful. Owning our toxic side, the mistakes made, let the cat out of the bag. When there is nothing to hide, we stop hiding. If you have never done this kind of work, telling your story can feel like climbing Mount Everest in a swimsuit. Not fun! They're just emotions, lovely humans. They're just emotions. I said it best in Chapter Two.

The things we face, we embrace.
The things we ignore, we store.
Empty the shelves.

Your narrative may not include deep wounds and long-buried shame. Or, perhaps, your version is far less traumatic. Masks are masks. Everyone benefits from stepping out of the shadows. And who among us has not made serious mistakes? Speaking your truth is a central concept to being Black Sheep Proud™.

It's important to share your story with a person or group that has no vested interest in the outcome. Tap into the type of unbiased acceptance that alters how you view yourself. I have experienced such a transformation, as have many others. Your story bears witness to the price paid, no longer concealed, your truth fully revealed. Scars worn with pride, eyes opened wide, you walk with wisdom. You are different than the crowd. That's a good thing! It's time to speak up. Gift your story to the world. Come out of the closet.

ESSAY #2: MAKE PEACE

Your story told, your truth spoken, it can take a minute or two to land on solid ground. What defines you? What needs to stay, and what needs to go? Wiser, less afraid, gutsier, it's time to make peace with the world.

Telling your story sets the stage.
Making peace claims the prize.

When mistakes you've made feel like a sledgehammer to the gut, that's a problem. When numbing out is so pronounced that only a dense fog remains, you stay stuck. When feeling small is a familiar song, mute the music! Toxic thinking is never a viable option.

Devastating shit happens, and there is nothing we can do about that reality. It's a bit ironic. We are powerless over being powerless! But it's true! Blaming God. Fighting the world. It's wasted energy. Believe me, I speak from experience. Moving forward requires letting go. One of the most famous prayers of all time is The Serenity Prayer, written in the 1800s by Reinhold Neibuhr. The short version commonly used by 12 Step groups speaks directly to the topic of making peace.

"God grant me the serenity to accept the things
I cannot change; courage to change the things I can;
and wisdom to know the difference."

In twenty-five words, we find everything we need to make peace with ourselves. It's all there, accepting our powerlessness, owning our power, and the need for discernment each step of the way. If God is not your jam, pop in the Higher Power of your choosing. It can be anything or anyone, as long as it's not you! Why is that important? Surrender only works when we surrender to a power greater than ourselves.

Life is not the enemy.
Make peace with life.

I have wanted to change my legal name for decades. It did not happen until age fifty-eight. The name I was born with, inherited from my biological father, is not the one on the book cover. Changing my last name to Ford in honor of my beloved grandmother was a way to reclaim my identity. I refuse to be defined by the trauma of my past or the brokenness of my parents. I am more than my scars. My life and identity are my own.

Deep healing has a voice.
Listen to the voice.

We all come from different places. My story and life experience may be radically different than your saga. Still, I have yet to meet a person who did not need to make peace with various aspects of their life. Everyone struggles.

As a reminder, we're in this together. Remember that from Chapter One? I meant it! I'm not a guru, and I damn sure don't have all the answers. If anyone acts as though they do, avoid them like the plague!

DUDE, CHILL OUT!

Please don't move on to the next section. Instead, take a few days off. Letting an experience marinate unlocks deeper levels of insight. It's just how our brains are wired. Our minds can only process so much at one time. As well, grabbing some R&R gives us a chance to reset. When doing intense work, catching our breath is crucial.

In some ways, this chapter may be the toughest in the book. Am I worthy? Am I good enough? Exploring those questions taps into some of our deepest insecurities. Good self-care is essential when traveling through rough terrain.

Downtime is not busy, numb, or work to the bone time. Celebrate your victories! Do things that soothe your soul, and restore your energy. If you need to add extra layers of self-care during this part of the journey, please do so. Be good to yourself! Honor your work by taking a break. Rest stops are a good thing.

AM I GOOD ENOUGH?

The doubts never entirely go away. Such is the journey, the price we pay. It's hard to believe that we have what it takes, the value the world needs. We itch for proof. The greater our insecurities, the greater our need for validation. Validate my decisions, success, value, looks, wealth, sex appeal, food choices, and life choices! Feed me validation! Homie needs validation! An addiction such as this is insatiable. It's a battle we can never win.

Step off the battlefield.
Exit the loop.

Being "good enough" is rooted in false gods whose dark magic is self-doubt. Yes, we do things right, but honestly, we're always falling short. Step up your game! Ugh. It's total crap. There is a vast difference between continual growth and an obligation to constantly measure up. The pursuit of "good enough" is a fool's errand.

In 2003, I crash-landed into AA. I had spent decades in the rooms with Bill's wife but never with Bill, the program that started it all. It was important that I dress for the occasion. Right? Dress to impress! Looking back, it's hilarious. Early in my sobriety, I heard someone say, "my very best shit got me here." It hit like a shotgun blast to the chest! Not long after, I stopped trying to be "good enough" for my AA tribe. Tis true. The best humor is found in real life.

I spent almost four years with Bill learning how to be a functional adult. As it turns out, I do not have the allergy that is alcoholism. I'm a generalist. Hell, I can become addicted to damn near anything! Numb at ninety will always be there, calling me out by name, desperately trying to fuck up my life. But more than anything, I think the rooms were a safe place to have a lovely nervous breakdown. I was in bad shape! No, joke. That incredible community saved my life. I will be forever grateful.

There is little to prove.

There is much to learn.

Will I ever get to the point where I don't have to deal with my demons? No, that will never happen. Do those demons hold the same sway as once they did? No, thank Yoda, they've been voted off the island. The problem is the bastards refuse to leave! So they do their thing, and I do mine. Most of the time, I come out on top. As far as I'm concerned, that's a win.

ESSAY #1: NAME YOUR VAMPIRES

Never feeling good enough on an irrational level is like being a vampire. We're always hungry! The need to feed never ends. The unrelenting obligation to be more creates an insatiable thirst for affirmation. When nothing fills the void, our world rapidly spins out of control.

I need to be better, stronger, wealthier, sexier, smarter like that person I know. Comparison shopping never leaves you whole! Intense insecurity makes for a potent poison. It shows no mercy, and no one is immune. I have witnessed it take down the best among us. Left to its own devices, this type of insecurity can make otherwise sane people do crazy ass things. It always brings out the worst in us because it plays into our deepest doubts.

Introspection breeds calm.
Avoidance breeds chaos.

Everyone struggles with insecurities, and the need for validation is normal. The problem occurs when the vampire stirs. How to tell the two apart? When insecurities are kicking your ass, you lose control. A button gets pushed, and suddenly logic goes out the window. It's like a panic attack on steroids. You get lost in a sea of reactions that can manifest in any number of ways. I'm reminded of the date gone wrong story I shared earlier.

As a reminder, we're exploring tender territory. If you find this topic triggering, take a break! Above all, don't shame yourself. That only makes it worse.

I have no family tree. Put another way, there is no plan B because that has never been an option. I've lived most of my life without a safety net. It's on me to stay above water. It's a heavy burden to bear. It's also terrifying at times. While many good things have come from my forced independence, there is a downside. When my security is threatened, for a brief moment, I lose my shit. The result is a rampaging vampire. Good times! As a result, I must be ever mindful of my behavior when triggered. Keeping a few blood bags in the refrigerator is super helpful. I'm kidding! Slurp. What?

Awareness fuels prevention.
Numbness fuels disaster.

Define your crazy. And to be clear, everyone has their version of crazy! It's urban slang, not a mental health dig. What triggers your deepest insecurities? What happens when you irrationally lose your shit? Don't be polite! Own your inner gunk! Puke it up, but don't beat yourself up. Everyone fights these battles. The important thing is to own your stuff. That's the only way anything changes.

ESSAY#2: KNOW YOUR VALUE

Whispers of self-doubt undermine our progress. The tendency to compensate rather than contemplate is strong. I'm not enough! I need to be more! Conclusions built on delusion. Nothing adds to nor diminishes your value. You live and learn, feel strong, then yearn, feel weak, then climb. To live is to have value. No matter your mistakes, that's all it takes. Your humanity is your salvation. The highs and lows are the journey.

Earlier, I wrote of false gods whose dark magic is self-doubt. But who, exactly, are these false gods? You will find these saboteurs in popularity contests, social media algorithms, trauma binds, TV commercials, social bias, peer pressure, oppression, and other insidious nooks. Silence the dark whispers! Detox from the doom scroll! Facilitate an existence that leaves you whole.

It's your story.
Take control of the narrative.

Several decades ago, an acquaintance confessed that while she would love to play matchmaker, the task was ill-fated. I was too authentic! How was she going to find someone that real? She was not trying to be mean. We had a ton of fun together. One evening, we almost got kicked out of a symphony performance. Who knew that was a thing? We made it a thing!

#BlackSheepProud
PS: I love the symphony.

My friend's confession speaks to a cloaked cancer in modern society. From a very young age, we are taught to be someone other than ourselves. True, authenticity has become all the rage. The younger generations give me hope. And yet, we still struggle to cope, feel, and heal while keeping it real. The constant need for validation outside ourselves traps us in a loop that gives away our power. We're not talking about an innocuous topic. We're talking about who gets to determine our value as human beings! I said it best in Chapter Two. It bears repeating (with a slight tweak).

Your value is your own.
Bring it back home!

FYI, feeling worthy or good enough will remain elusive if you destroy your life with reckless abandon. One might think this is obvious. Not so much! The antidote never works if you keep drinking poison. The solution? Stop drinking poison! If that requires professional help, so be it. Do whatever it takes to *stay* on solid ground.

One of the things I hear from couples that have been married for decades is that while they always love their spouse, there are times they don't much like their spouse. For me, this gets to the essence of valuing oneself. While I value myself, there are times when I don't much like the person in the mirror. Similar to a marriage, it's a give-and-take process. When I make a grave mistake, it pisses me off! Forgiveness doesn't happen overnight, and I'm grateful for this tendency. It keeps me honest.

Owning your value requires self-empathy without prerequisites. We all make mistakes, some with lifelong consequences. We all do things we wish we could take back. Our value is not a calculation of wins and losses or good deeds versus bad deeds. Our value is our humanity.

That's it.
Keep it simple.
Mic Drop!

DUDE, CHILL OUT! (THE SEQUEL)

Please don't jump into the journaling section just yet. Instead, take a few days off. As a reminder, letting an experience marinate unlocks deeper levels of insight. Secondly, grabbing some R&R gives us a chance to reset. Practicing good self-care is essential when traveling through rough terrain.

Downtime is not busy, numb, or work to the bone time. Celebrate your victories! Do things that soothe your soul, and restore your energy. If you need to add extra layers of self-care during this journey, please do so. Be good to yourself! Honor your work by taking time off.

IT'S THE LITTLE THINGS

I have never lost the playfulness that comes with being a child. No matter how old I get, my childlike curiosity remains. A life without wonder is no life at all, in my view. I seek it out wherever it might be found! As a result, my laugh is more of a wild cackle. Then there is my life as a geek. Where to begin? As a lifelong fan of all things sci-fi, fantasy, and otherworldly, it's a big part of my jam. I once wrote a Star Wars blog post about *The Force Awakens* that got over 230,000 reads! My claim to geek fame. Clearly, I'm rocking some epic Force Power.

Owning our quirks connects us to the Black Sheep part of ourselves. We're different. That's ok. Even awesome. It's a way to honor our worth as unconventional beings to whatever degree you view yourself as such.

Assignment #1 / What quirky little things make you, well, you? Please, do not judge or edit your responses. Go for broke. Burn down the closet! Rip off the mask. When you're done, check in with a few of your closest friends. What quirky little things do they like about you? The reason this exercise is powerful is it blasts past our walls. The result is an authentic snapshot of our persona, free from societal expectations and peer pressure.

CONTEMPLATIVE JOURNALING
Honor Your Humanity

To embrace your humanity is to embrace the fact life is messy and you are imperfect. By giving yourself grace, and plenty of space, you validate your existence versus seeking approval externally.

1) Create a title page. Write Life Choice #2, and then a few spaces below, write, Honor your Humanity. Dress up the page with graphics if that's your thing. Make this contemplative session your own!

2) Add a few pages of actionable insights from this chapter. An insight is actionable when it moves you to act in a specific way. Earlier, I wrote, "Surf your rough edges. Find your sane." If I were reading versus writing this book, I would explore those edges deeply to find my sane. Look for insights that inspire you to act!

HABIT #1: STAND IN YOUR TRUTH

Sharing your story and making peace is a release from the bondage of societal expectations. There is nothing to hide! In stepping out of the shadows, you reclaim your truth. Where to begin? Here are a few ideas to get you started.

Get Help / Unconditional self-acceptance is never easy. Encouraging words lighten the load. Powerful insights show the way. Get the help you need from a therapist, support group, and/or recovery community.

Where does it hurt?
You're not alone.

Break It Down / Survival was the central theme of my life for the first twenty years. Success for the next twenty, then meaning. Life is not a continuous novel. It's several, each connected but with its own premise. Break down your life into eras to connect the dots.

Identify the themes.
Document your evolution.

Let Go / The weight of carrying rocks exacts a heavy toll. At some point, we have to empty the backpack. Making peace trades hate for healing and acting out for effective action. Where do you need to let go? How will you make that happen? Stop collecting rocks!

Holding on keeps us stuck.
Letting go sets us free.

3) Set aside twenty pages to work on the first habit. Use the first page of this habit as the title page. Write, "Honor Your Humanity: Habit #1 - Stand In Your Truth." Add graphics and visuals if that's your thing. Make it your own!

4) How to get better at standing in your truth? What action steps need to happen? Make it real. Be specific. Develop a new habit. As a reminder, Rome was not built in a day. Progress, not perfection.

HABIT #2: STAND IN YOUR POWER

We stand in our power when we look upon the imperfect, epic, broken, yet beautiful soul in the mirror and say, "I got your back." Unconditional Self-acceptance makes for good medicine. Take your medicine!

Create Context / What does healthy validation, internal or otherwise, look like in your life? Please, be specific. What does toxic validation look like in your life? Please, be specific. Cite examples. Paint a picture.

Own your value.
Embrace your imperfections.

Avoid Landmines / What builds you up, and what takes you down? The evidence is all around. Examine the evidence! What builds your self-worth? What erodes your self-worth? Follow the clues. Dig deep.

Scale your confidence.
Prevent self-sabotage.

Ratify Your Non-Compliance / Push back against the things that don't feel right. Claim your independence! Have you connected with your tribe? Where do you need to assert yourself?

Reject oppression.
Embrace your truth.

5) Set aside twenty pages to work on the second habit. Use the first page of this habit as the title page. Write, "Honor Your Humanity: Habit #2 - Stand In Your Power." Add graphics and visuals if that's your thing. Make it your own!

6) How can you get better at standing in your power? What resources do you need? What action steps need to happen? Make it real. Be specific. Develop a new habit. As a reminder, Rome was not built in a day. Be gentle with yourself! Progress, not perfection.

7) Celebrate! It's not easy to do this kind of work, but it is worthwhile. You are investing in yourself! You are learning to own your Black Sheep voice and powers. Do something nice for yourself. Get in the habit of celebrating your victories, large and small.

How to accept yourself as you are with no pre-conditions, escape clauses, or awkward pauses when someone compliments you from the heart? You are legit, even if you could be more. There is always more, but for today, you're doing just fine.

Honor your humanity!

CHAPTER #4

OWN YOUR SKIN

71

"To be yourself in a world that is constantly trying to make you something else is the greatest accomplishment."

Ralph Waldo Emerson

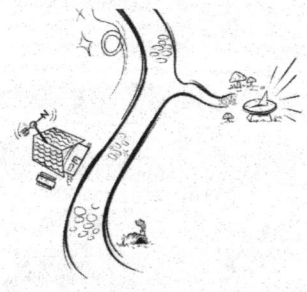

Be the bull that wanders glasshouses. Flip apple carts with pride. Whisper less. Say more. Put your words to good use! Live by a code. Remain flexible. Have a vision. Make decisions. Mistakes, too! Rock your edge. Create earthquakes. Or, perhaps your jam is inward, awkward, with a side of daydreaming? Equally epic. And hey, the best version is the imperfect version.

Ladies and Gents, step right up! One size fits all! The rusty conveyor belt moans, groans, and clanks as it churns. Don't let it silence the passions that burn! Jump off the conveyor belt. Reject the status quo. Travel True North. Blaze your own trail.

How to package your persona as a Black Sheep being? Burn the institutional gift wrap. Dump the labels. Personal branding? Meh! Having a distinct point of view? Yes! Doubling down on the projects that speak to your soul? Now we're talking! The best roadmap is the one you already own.

Traits and quirks hidden in shame only cause pain. Own your skin. Be yourself without hesitation or apology. Choose your fate. Ignore the hate. The secret to soulful success is found in the mirror. Know thyself. Walk thy path. Learn as you go. Take notes. Use your notes. By the way, you hold the power! Use it wisely.

BLACK SHEEP DNA

I turn sixty in less than a year. My unruly response to aging is predictable. Know your limits? Not a chance! Although my collarbone is completely detached from my left shoulder, I still give the treadmill hell three times a week. When surgery repairs the break, I'll return to the modified HIIT training I love. The intensity and drive rarely subside! But I have my moments.

The photoshoot for my book and marketing materials had to capture the real me. Hiding the toll of my Black Sheep life was never an option. Ok, a few touch-ups, but nothing too radical. Photoshoots have never triggered anxiety in the past, but this one had me whirling! Why am I stressing out? Vulnerability can be a transformative experience. It also feels like drowning.

Brio Cooney, a dear friend and the photographer, held space for my anxiety. She didn't try to fix me. Rather, she gave me breathing room to blossom. It was an intense shoot, four hours nonstop. Tears were shed. Tender moments were shared. When the photos arrived, I felt ancient and then pride. I was unwilling to hide. My story is found in the lines on my face. Hello, Bobby Ford! To truly see ourselves, we must open our eyes.

ESSAY#1: NON-COMPLIANCE

It rarely happens in an instant. It builds over time. Inch by inch, you declare your independence. Obscure twentieth-century Poet Muriel Strode wrote, "I will not follow where the path may lead, but I will go where there is no path, and I will leave a trail." The quote, incorrectly attributed to Emerson, is nutrient-rich for the Black Sheep of the world. Obedience never breeds joy for our kind. And yet, the pressure to fit in never ends. Kiss the ring. Stay in your lane. Be well behaved. Seriously? Slam on the brakes! It's your damn car. Anyone that doesn't get that can get out and walk!

Non-compliance is a choice.
Make the choice.

Carve out your place in the world. Flesh out your brand of bliss. It is in the act of rebellion that we find our way. Ratify your non-compliance. Travel unknown roads. Be gentle with yourself when you crash. Celebrate the victories. Enjoy the ride.

One defining trait of non-compliance is rejecting or altering the traditional way of doing things. The typical approach is rarely our approach when a project, topic, or cause triggers our deepest passions. As noted in Chapter Two, the established method for writing a book shut me down. Had I attempted to comply, the result would have been words that tasted like sun-baked cardboard. Hungry for another dry morsel, are ya? And that assumes I could have written a book at all, which I seriously doubt. Without inspiration, staying the course is unlikely.

The danger, of course, is non-compliance that is forced or disingenuous. It never works. Pushing the envelope is not about our egos. It's about who we are as people and how we go about doing our work or craft. It's in our DNA. It's how our brains are wired. As an aside, my version of pounding my own drum is different than your version. Each individual must find their own path.

ESSAY#2: INTENSITY

Black Sheep typically bring hurricane levels of intensity to their lives, work, and craft. While that intensity is our bread and butter, we must be careful. Our kinetic energy can be as destructive as it is transformative. Surf your rough edges! Also, being intense has nothing to do with introversion or extroversion. Our intensity is born from strong passions, opinions, values and the like. It can be a bit much, even for ourselves!

Start wildfires.
Control the burn.

What will be my legacy? A gear turns, then another, followed by a loud pop-click! It's time to write a book. Will anyone read it? Pop-click! Writing floods me. I'm drowning in emotion. Pop-click! Pen to the page. Crazy highs and lows. My passion burns until the last gear turns. Pop-click! Holy crap, I wrote a book!

Intense fears. Shove them into a box. Maybe one day? Definitely, not today. A gear turns, then another, followed by a loud pop-click! All hell breaks loose. Nothing makes sense. Something has to give. Pop-click! Crash, then soar, then crash again. Lessons learned. A fresh start grabs hold. Pop-click! Chaos remains but in a controlled, dare I say, productive way? The last gear turns. Pop-click! The storm subsides. I'm still alive. Perhaps, even a bit wiser.

Managing our intensity requires paying attention. It's easy to race past essential details and warning signs. When we do, we sabotage our own success. We must practice patience, give grace, and plenty of space to the person in the mirror. How to cuddle with a fire-breathing dragon?

ESSAY #3: ROUGH EDGES

Slam a shot of obsession. Toke some weird. Drop a few hits of imagination. Enjoy the ride. It's a righteous high! Recreational drugs? Nope! It's a peek inside the Black Sheep creative process. The world struggles to understand *heightened people* who create on the very edge of traditional realities. What in the hell is wrong with you? Absolutely nothing! Why are you so fracking strange? Try to keep up! Why rock the boat? Fasten your seat belt! We each have our own process. Your rituals may or may not be as heightened as your peers. It matters not. Rock your own rodeo.

Behaviors classified as extreme include some of our best Black Sheep traits. Obsessed, eccentric, odd, rebellious, weird, wild, playful, geeky, nerdy, and other quirks deliver the fire we need to succeed. Absent that edge, we become generic. Flat. Bland, at best.

Add fuel to your fire!
Burn bright without apology.

The line between healthy obsession and the kind that burns the damn house down is paper thin. Pick any edge trait deemed valuable by you and excessive by others. The potential for harm likely exists. Keep it real. Find your center. Don't drown! Rough edges only serve your life if they're not destroying your life. Right? Are you laughing right now? Self-awareness is key, as is personal accountability. If you're circling the drain or blowing up your life, please stop pretending otherwise. Hit the pause button. You can change the world down the road. Know when to go fast and when to go slow.

ESSAY #4: UNCONDITIONAL TRUST

All alone on a stage up high. No audience. No cast or crew. Just you, standing in the spotlight. You're there for a reason. Embrace the project, passion, or obsession that has taken over your mind! Walking away leads to mountains of regret. Make a calculated bet. For better or worse, go all in until you win. That's the rodeo.

Trust yourself.
Take a leap of faith.

Imagine being flamboyant, larger-than-life Elton John before he became a household name. How to trust yourself when the world does not get you? Imagine being Dr. Martin Luther King Jr. before he became a celebrated activist. How to trust yourself when the world violently attacks your message at every turn?

Trust your identity. The traits that are core. Trust your instincts as proven over time. Trust your experience as the wisdom that you have earned. Trust your talents, especially those that don't fit in a box. You are the Secret Sauce! You are the thunder that shatters the status quo.

Ignore the critics.
Be the wildcard.

Owning your skin is unconditionally trusting yourself just as you are without pre-conditions. Let that sink in for a moment or two. Do you trust yourself, personally or professionally, when it matters the most? Playing it safe when feeling insecure, while understandable, tosses you in a jail cell of your own design. Doubling down on your work or craft is crucial. The same with your Black Sheep vibe. Failure is given. Heed Beckett's sage advice. Fail more! Fail better! As you gain experience being yourself and doing your thing, it gets easier to trust your talents and instincts. It becomes automatic. Translation? Jump in the deep end! Confidence is born of experience.

ESSAY #5: THE LONG GAME

When recovering from general anesthesia, I wake up far earlier than expected. My subconscious mind perceives being sedated as a severe threat. As a result, even though I'm out cold, my blood pressure skyrockets from what amounts to an unconscious panic attack. Extreme fight-or-flight reactions are rare, but they still happen. A part of me remains ever fearful of the next traumatic event. Progress, not perfection.

Doing visionary work or craft is the lifeblood of Black Sheep, but here is the reality check. Nothing happens overnight! The same with our personal battles. Growth takes years, even decades.

Practice patience.
Play the long game.

The original budget for the hit indie movie "Once" was one million dollars, with Cillian Murphy attached to the lead role. When he opted out, the funding dried up. Writer/Director John Carney recruited fellow musicians to star in the film, which he made for a little under $140K before finishing funds. A project is considered low budget when its funding is below $7 million!

The odds against such a film winning an Oscar for best song, getting a Grammy nomination, becoming a musical, and ending up in a Simpson's episode are astronomical! The list of Black Sheep ventures that have beat similar odds is endless. And yet, fame and fortune are rarely the sought prize.

Owning your skin is the willingness to stay the course. Sure, the math may not be in your favor. Cut a path! Change the math! But know this, the journey takes time.

HELP IS ON THE WAY

In 2018, Richard Stanton and John Volanthen, two world-renown British cave divers, rescued water utility workers from a flooded cave complex in Thailand. Although a quick rescue, it was challenging. The workers panicked while briefly underwater, wrestling with the divers. Twelve members of a local football team, all teenagers, and their coach had yet to be found. It was not looking good.

Almost a week after the initial rescue, two and a half miles into the submerged cave complex, Stanton and Volanthen located the trapped football team. The group was huddled on a small mound of rock. The oxygen level was 15%, several points below the level required to sustain life. The clock was ticking.

If the utility workers could not handle using a regulator for a few minutes, the famed divers reasoned, attempting additional rescues would prove impossible. United States Air Force MSgt. Derek Anderson pushed back, "What does doing the impossible look like?"

The team recruited Dr. Richard Harris, an experienced cave diver and anesthesiologist, to do the unthinkable. Under general anesthesia, while wearing dive gear, the teens would be sedated and submerged, unconscious, in the water. A lone diver would guide each teen back to the mouth of the cave one child at a time. Nothing like this had ever been done. The chance of catastrophe was high.

The journey took up to three hours to complete per rescue. The dive team had to learn how to sedate the teens because the anesthesia wore off before they got to safety. The only way to know if a boy was breathing was the bubbles that emitted from the child's dive mask! Parts of the cave were so narrow that only one person could pass at a time. Making matters worse, the water visibility was close to zero. A million things could have gone wrong!

The entire football team and their coach were rescued. Sadly, former Thai Navy SEAL Saman Kunan lost his life in the effort. His widow captured the importance of her husband's sacrifice and the international effort with just three words.

"Generosity is everything."

Why share this story? In the National Geographic documentary, *The Rescue*, Richard Stanton, John Volanthen, Dr. Richard Harris, and other divers shared their lifelong struggles with being Black Sheep. They were not popular kids while growing up. Several were bullied in their youth and anti-social as adults. Stanton is uncomfortable around kids. Do all Black Sheep struggle with these issues? Of course not. The pain of being different manifests in many ways. But pain is pain.

One of my favorite quotes from the film is when Dr. Harris proudly states, "Last to be chosen for the cricket team, first to be chosen for the cave rescue!" Thirteen people, most teenagers, would have perished had an eclectic group of Black Sheep not answered the call.

FEARLESS

People view me as fearless. When you get comfortable in your own skin, in my experience, you tend to take more risks. Huh? Owning your skin requires trusting yourself, which puts more options on the table. Taking action from a place of self-trust is vastly different than the superficial bravado marketed as being fearless. Authentic, steadfast resolve does not sway with the wind.

When I owned an ad agency, my fees included a large initial retainer and a monthly fee for our ongoing services. A multi-state retailer had paid us for the initial discovery process but was unwilling to commit beyond the initial gig. The discovery process culminated in a retreat where I shared my findings.

After our retreat, the client plopped several large three-ring binders on the conference table with a loud thud. Each meaty binder was a pitch from a competitor. The client wanted to give us a leg up on the competition. I paused in silence for a brief moment, then tossed each presentation into the trash, one beefy binder at a time.

Audacity makes for good medicine.
A little goes a long way!

I knew we hit it out of the park in the discovery phase. Dealing with the elephant in the room was the only viable option. I catered their lunch, shared my point of view, then gave them two hours to decide. It was now or never! They signed on and remained a loyal client for many years. Was I being fearless? No, I was not.

My reaction was principled and backed by decades of experience. I took an informed risk because I trusted myself. Are you at peace with making informed True North decisions, regardless of where the chips might land?

When Richard Stanton, the cave diver, was asked to transport bracelets a monk had blessed to the trapped football team, he angrily threw them to the ground! After a bit of prodding, he relented and delivered them to the teens. Imperfect people with intense emotions do incredible things all the time! Being bold despite your baggage is a proud Black Sheep tradition.

Trust your truth.
Find power in your principles.

Soulful success has little to do with the absence of fear. If anything, fear is used as a catalyst to inform and even elevate work or craft. In the fire, we find the fuel! Plant your brand of seed to grow your kind of crop. Owning your skin makes for good soil.

CRAFT YOUR AVATAR

Getting in touch with the Black Sheep part of yourself can be challenging if the concept is new. In my case, being an outlier is hard to miss! It's baked into my story. Even so, coming face-to-face with myself as I wrote this book has been challenging. Meaning, I get it. To get the most from this exercise, surrender to an environment conducive to this kind of soulful exploration. Please work on your avatar uninterrupted for the best results.

Prepare The Canvas / You'll need a large piece of paper for this exercise, such as a flip chart or a large sketch pad. At the top center of the worksheet, write - My Black Sheep Avatar. In the middle of your canvas, dead center, create a circle big enough to hold your first and last name. When you're done, add your name to the circle.

Create a worksheet that has four workspaces of equal size. To accomplish this, focus on the circle in the middle containing your name. Draw a vertical line from the top of the circle to the Black Sheep Avatar title. Draw a vertical line from the bottom of the circle to the bottom of the page. On the left-hand side of the circle, draw a horizontal line to the left end of the page. On the right-hand side of the circle, draw a horizontal line to the right end of the page.

The result should be a canvas with a title at the top, four empty boxes of equal size, and a circle in the middle with your name. If that is (mostly) what you're seeing, please move on to the next part of the exercise. If not, revisit the instructions. Remember, it doesn't need to be perfect.

Identity - The Top Left Box / Put the title of this section along with your answers in the top left box. As a reminder, you're just creating a snapshot. Please don't overthink this exercise. Enjoy the process.

How do you identify as a human being? Note your preferred pronoun and five words (not a sentence, just words) that best capture your persona. Remember, perfection is not the goal!

How would you describe your look? This question has zero to do with societal constructs of attractiveness and everything to do with your personality. How do you manifest your persona? What are the hallmarks of your look? Have fun with this question.

How would you describe your lifestyle? Avoid superficial measurements. What's your jam? How do you spend your time? Zero in on the rituals and passions that define your existence. Lifestyles have a vibe. Clarify that vibe.

What are the hallmark traits of your personality? This question has nothing to do with the compliments you receive and *everything* to do with the things you love about yourself. Please don't rush this question!

Rough Edges - The Top Right Box / Put the title of this section along with your answers in the top right box. As a reminder, you're just creating a snapshot. Please don't overthink this exercise. Enjoy the process!

What rough edges have served you well over the years? This exercise may prove challenging if you have not embraced this part of yourself. Start small. Identify five to seven unconventional behaviors/traits that have helped you out over the years. For example, I've never been one to seek the approval of others. What you see is what you get.

Why did you pick a given rough edge? How does it manifest in your life? What has been the positive impact of this maverick trait or behavior in your life? Embrace your rough edges!

Truth - The Lower Left Box / Put the title of this section along with your answers in the lower left box. As a reminder, you're just creating a snapshot. Please don't overthink this exercise. Enjoy the process!

What is the logline for the movie about your life? A logline is a single-sentence description of a movie. My film's logline might be "A traumatized boy fights impossible odds, rising from the ashes to live a creative life of impact and meaning." Notice how it only takes a few words to effectively communicate the essence of my story? As a reminder, please don't overthink this exercise. Enjoy the process! Your logline does not need to be perfect, but it does need to be honest.

What are the big lessons of your life thus far? This book is chalked full of lessons learned. But if I had to boil them all down to the big ones, six come to mind: embrace the struggle, honor your humanity, own your skin, feed your soul, meet the moment, and make rain. Does any of that sound familiar? It does not matter if you are eighteen or eighty. Lessons have been learned! Pick the top five to ten to keep this simple.

What values and principles inform your life daily? I recommend doing a little online research to clarify, in your mind, the difference between values and principles. A few of my values are freedom, humor, and passion. Speaking truth to power, shattering the status quo, and doing right by people are principles central to my life. Keep it simple! You only need a glimpse for this exercise to be compelling.

Power - The Lower Right Box / Put the title of this section along with your answers in the lower right box. As a reminder, you're just creating a snapshot. Please don't overthink this exercise. Enjoy the process!

Accomplishments are not exclusive to your work or craft. Raising your kids to be healthy, happy human beings could top the list. Studying abroad, surviving a rough divorce, or backpacking across Europe are but a few possible options. While proud of my business career, my creative work brought meaning to my life. What accomplishments fill you with pride? This section is solely about your point of view.

What are your top five talents? Mine *probably* include being fully present, making big things happen, touching people's lives, pushing the envelope, and something around ideation. It's tempting to get crazy anal on this exercise. Are those *really* my top five? Even as I write this, the talent question wants to pull me into cavernous rabbit holes! Keep it simple. Avoid perfection.

Instincts are primal and innate to our core self. For example, I'm an off-the-charts empath that can rapidly read people. I also spot bullshit a mile away. These instincts are common among survivors of childhood trauma. I also have strong instincts in the business and creative worlds based on many years of experience in those fields. What primal instincts have served you well throughout your life? Please try to be specific.

What has been the tangible impact of your life, work, and craft over the years? Minimizing the significance of your existence is not an option! The vanilla, mind-blowing, and everywhere in-between impact adds up! Every contribution matters. All of it has value. Social media posts that make the world a better place are no different than winning a Grammy. What? You have clearly lost your mind, Bobby Ford! Seriously, at the end of the day, it's all relative. Clarify the impact you have had on the world.

Ponder & Process / After completing your Black Sheep Avatar, tuck it away for a week or two. Let it marinate. When you return, review your work. Add visuals and polish if so inclined. Please avoid dragging this exercise out. The goal is not to perfectly capture every aspect of your Black Sheep. You're creating an inspired snapshot.

Create a private, *meditative space* that will allow you to disappear from the world. Light comfort food and drink at the ready. Mood music softly plays in the background. Candles or incense might happen, depending upon your tastes. Your laptop or journal is within arms reach. Sacred work requires an environment that honors that work.

When you look at your avatar, who do you see? What stands out? What immediately comes to mind? What realizations appear? Where do you need to double down? If tears well up, listen to your tears. Judge nothing. Embrace everything. Learn to reverently walk with yourself as a talented, Black Sheep being.

An obsession for greatness, wealth, or fame, whatever the hunger, the addiction is the same. The external world holds all the cards! Take back your power! Deal from your own deck. The person whose approval matters the most is found in the mirror. See yourself clear. Cherish the value that is unique to you alone.

CONTEMPLATIVE JOURNALING
Own Your Skin

Owning your skin is a choice to be yourself without hesitation or apology. The good and not-so-good. The edge that gives you an edge. The best skin to wear is the one that already exists.

1) Create a title page. Write Life Choice #3, and then a few spaces below, write, Own Your Skin. Dress up the page with graphics if that's your thing. Make this contemplative session your own!

2) Add a few pages of actionable insights from this chapter. An insight is actionable when it moves you to act in a specific way. Earlier, we worked on your Black Sheep Avatar. If I were reading versus writing this book, I would focus on my avatar. Where am I still hiding? Look for insights that inspire you to act!

HABIT #1: SPEAK YOUR TRUTH

When silence sparks suffering, silence is not an option. Step out of the shadows! Be messy, awesome, put together, and perfectly incomplete. Speaking your truth is an act of personal integrity. Where to begin? Here are a few ideas to help you get started!

Own Your Avatar / It is one thing to use your words. It's another thing to speak from a place of purpose and truth. How to better own your skin in everyday life? How to be your version of loud and proud?

Reveal your authentic self.
Give it room to run.

Share Your Journey / Who are you when fully revealed? What stories do you have to share? And to whom will you share your story? Vulnerable truths speak louder than well-crafted words.

What keeps you invisible?
Burn down the closet!

Preach Your Gospel / A message with meaning, unrelenting, occasionally screaming. You have thoughts to share. What do you have to say to the world? Why should they listen?

Grab a megaphone!
Share your truth.

3) Set aside twenty pages to work on the first habit. Use the first page of this habit as the title page. Write, "Own Your Skin: Habit #1 - Speak Your Truth."Add graphics and

visuals if that's your thing. Make it your own! Have fun with the process.

4) How to get better at speaking your truth? What resources do you need? What action steps need to happen? Make it real. Be specific. Develop a new habit. As a reminder, Rome was not built in a day. Be gentle with yourself! Progress, not perfection.

HABIT #2: DOUBLE DOWN

Your spoken truth reveals the ideals that inform your life. And yet, you remain dormant unless you act! Owning your skin is a verb, not a noun. Double down! Where to begin? Here are a few ideas to help you get started!

Get Involved / Connect with like-minded people. Find the tribes that bring you to life! Get involved with groups, hobbies, causes, projects, and anything that empowers your path. Where to begin? Start a list!

Stretch your wings.
Jump out of the nest!

Stand Your Ground / Speak up, and act out! Let people know what you believe, the things you are trying to achieve, and the injustice that cannot stand. Where do you need to assert boundaries? Where do you need to pump up the volume?

Draw a line in the sand.
Claim your land!

Steel Your Resolve / Trust the value you bring to the world. Pursue the projects you feel called to do. What will it take for you to play the long game? How can you strengthen your resolve?

Process the pain.
Fight for the victories.

5) Set aside twenty pages to work on the second habit. Use the first page of this habit as the title page. Write, "Own Your Skin: Habit #2 - Double Down."Add graphics and visuals if that's your thing.

6) How can you get better at doubling down? What resources do you need? What action steps need to happen? Make it real. Be specific. Develop a new habit. As a reminder, Rome was not built in a day. Be gentle with yourself! Progress, not perfection.

7) Celebrate! It's not easy to do this kind of work, but it is worthwhile. You are investing in yourself! You are

learning to own your Black Sheep voice and powers. Do something nice for yourself. Get in the habit of celebrating your victories, large and small.

Be the bull that wanders glasshouses. Flip apple carts with pride. Whisper less. Say more. Put your words to good use! Live by a code. Remain flexible. Have a vision. Make decisions. Mistakes, too. Find your way. And hey, the best version is the imperfect version.

Own your skin!

DO YOUR THING

Visionary ideas? Give them life! Do you have what it takes? It's a question we all ask, which leads to the task of testing the water. Failure is a given. Success, too. You'll learn as you go. Keeping moving. Keep doing your thing. It gets better with time.

I have been a ravenous student of all things improbable my entire adult life. Sure, the origin story comes from my need to survive as a young lad. But my interest in pushing the envelope is fueled by the dance itself. The creative process is my drug of choice. Anything is possible! My brain lights up like a Christmas tree.

Ideas. Whims. Passions. Fleeting thoughts. Mild curiosities. Never-ending obsessions. Creating stuff. Breaking stuff. Thinking. Tinkering. Playing with fire. And then a lone spark lands. The first domino falls, and I am forever changed.

I guess that's why I watch so many documentaries about the visionaries that I admire. In getting to know the world's maestros as mere mortals, their brilliance and process feel accessible.

We cover a lot of territory in the next three chapters. Everything kicks up a notch! More exercises. More tangible tools. What can you do to make the most of the experience? Do the work! If you max out, take a break.

CHAPTER 5

FEED YOUR SOUL

"Walk as if you are kissing the earth with your feet."

Buddhist Monk Thích Nhất Hạnh

To soar in a society that feeds on superficial food is no easy task. The common good takes a backseat to greed with a side of grievance. Violence and hate fail to abate. Then a pandemic hits, and the need for meaning grows ever louder. How to find your way amid such stress? How to do your thing amid such strain?

Core to our being is seeing with all of our senses. The Fire Within is not visible to the naked eye. We are not the flesh and blood we wear outside. Our supernatural magic exists in another realm. When it's fed, we feel whole. But we rarely notice such moments. Slow down. Breathe. Reduce your speed. Connect with the part of yourself that operates behind the scenes.

True North is found using a compass only your soul can see. Walk barefoot in silence. Twirl in the pouring rain. Play with childlike glee. Surrender to a long embrace. Be less than perfect. Ask for help. Lend a hand. Chase a dream. Do your thing. Apologize. Then realize True North rarely screams. It's just something you know when the pace is slow.

Rush less.
Hear more.

MATTERS OF THE SOUL

Upon Googling "ikigai," you will be inundated with a popular Venn diagram that ignores the ancient word's true meaning. The framework transforms a thousand-year-old Japanese life philosophy into a prosperity hack. Remember that bit about feasting on superficial food? I'm all for prosperity! Hacking a culture's life philosophy, not so much. Master Yoda offers us much wisdom on the topic of ikigai in Star Wars: The Empire Strikes Back.

"Luminous beings are we,
not this crude matter."

The age-old Japanese concept of ikigai refers to a person's reason for being. Helping people, for example, is central to my ikigai, or my reason for being. What brings *tremendous meaning* to your life?

Many years ago, my hair stylist at the time recommended highlights. I had never color-treated my hair, so why not? It went terribly wrong! I ended up looking like Billy Idol with my hair bleached white. Which, if you're a rockstar, totally makes sense. I was a management consultant! There's a plot twist. The next day, I had to jump on a plane to do a speaking gig. Good times!

I was a road warrior back in the day. Free upgrades to First Class came with the job. Sitting next to me was a soft-spoken guy wearing a three-piece suit. I was the polar opposite. White hair, a baseball hat, and jeans gave me a retired boy band vibe. We struck up a conversation. Would he ask for my autograph? What if he asked me to sing? I can't sing!

After some chit-chat, I discovered my travel companion was a senior VP with a well-known international brand. On his business card was his full Japanese name. "You can call me Frank," he reassured. It's a standard business practice to make conversations easier for Westerners. We talked non-stop during the three-hour flight. It was a meaningful conversation. Long story short, we became penpals.

One of my favorite emails from Frank was about his family's rice farm that went back generations. He loved to bring in the harvest with his son each year, as was tradition. That would happen soon, he wrote. The image of father/son working rice paddies, as had been done for hundreds of years, was heart-warming.

Frank rushed less and heard more in life. Frank honored his ikigai. Rushing less (in this context) has nothing to do with reducing your workload. It has to do with being fully present. A soul-led life is a fully present life.

Ignore the distractions.
Cherish the journey.

FIND YOUR SOULFUL CENTER

Consciousness is the state of being aware, especially of something within oneself. Let's talk about coffee! Today, I ordered my usual dark roast with oat milk and Stevia. My gas gauge blinked amber when my car roared to life to pick up the black nectar of resurrection. Seriously? Do I get gas first, only to suffer a lukewarm cup of joe? Or do I go for broke, grab the coffee, and then get gas?

Every ounce of my being wanted to throw caution to the wind! I need dark java now! But then my "something within oneself" voice chimed in with a sardonic tone. "You know how this will end, Bobby? Coffee and no gas!" Sigh.

Temptation has your number.
Don't take the call!

Our Black Sheep nature is challenging. On the one hand, it helps us do visionary, kick-ass things. Our life experiences can be rich with meaning. On the other hand, as stated throughout this book, it can also burn your house down! How to play nice with a fire-breathing dragon?

Oneness / No matter how dark the darkness or insane the insanity, being at one with yourself offers peace and gives relief. A greater purpose is revealed. There is more to your story than meets the eye! How do you experience a deep sense of wholeness in your life? What *meaningfully anchors* your daily existence?

Oneness creates a calm resolve. It allows us to do more than merely survive. Find comfort in your humanity. You are a child of The Universe, God, whatever higher power works. Claiming your place in the world is a divine act.

Presence / How do you know your mind, body, and heart are fully present? What helps you stay in the moment? The magic of life is unfolding even as you read these words. Be aware of the world around you. Connect with the moments. Be fully present when engaged in conversations. Let life wash over you one precious second at a time.

When we live in the now, little gets past us. Each drop of existence, good or bad, offers value. To be fully aware is to be fully alive. Immerse yourself in the present tense. Live in the now!

Sustenance / How do you renew your physical being? How do you quiet your mind? How do you awaken your spirit? When food and drink are a source of strength, our vessel becomes our ally. When the mind is rested, well-fed, and on fire, we open doors once thought impossible. When we meditate or pray, we find peace. Rituals that nourish the soul plant deep roots.

I drink lots of water. Small dinner parties forge a sense of belonging. Real food gives me energy. Daydreams filled with magical worlds take me away. Music, silence, and crazy cold air set the stage for my meditations. Such are the routines that keep me whole. Know your hunger! Get fed in ways that work for you.

Sustain The Connection / Staying soulfully centered is the counterbalance to losing our way. It's a dependable guardian if we heed its counsel. How to do that if these concepts are new? Or, perhaps, you have already done significant inner work? Regardless of where you are on your journey, the three disciplines keep you on solid ground. That said, developing these habits is a process. Such is the journey. The price we pay to find peace.

In working on the final edits for this book, I revisit this section. The last few weeks have been brutal. To be honest, I am exhausted beyond measure. Monday, I surrender my baby, this manuscript, to the publisher. After a few days of much-needed rest, it will be time to return to the rituals that keep me whole. Everyone gets lost. The path remains.

PROTECT THE WIND

On my galleon, the Black Sheep flag hangs high. A lone finger probes the sky. Where might thy wind blow? Driven by forces I don't entirely understand. Born from a place true to my soul. I sail on the dice of chance to explore possibilities beyond my own. The wind that fills my sails blows True North. Still, on occasion, with no breeze, I sit alone on wide open seas.

Feelings like self-doubt, insecurity, and fear (just to mention a few) prevent us from unpacking our full potential. If we don't face these wind killers head-on, they flourish unabated. When toxic emotions get the best of us, they silence our soul's deepest yearnings.

In my early twenties, during a tough period in my life, a psychologist told me I had a pronounced gift for helping people. Helping people? Me? While I had a deep respect for the man, there was no way in hell I could ever help folks! Had he gone mad? He saw The Fire Within two decades before I claimed the mantle.

Numbing out has long been a lethal wind killer. If you find yourself stoned, drunk, or otherwise impaired without fail, there's a chance you're getting lit to tune out. Anything that is done in excess: booze, drugs, exercise, work, gaming, you name it, can be used to avoid the realities of life. We all need ways to escape, but if done without moderation, the wind disappears. All that remains is the soul-crushing silence of going through the motions.

Numb out less.
Protect the wind.

Self-sabotage is an even trickier wind killer because it often involves behaviors we don't immediately view as self-sabotage. Do you remember my story about trying to screw my way to never-ending bliss and confidence? How about my confession to being a lifelong workaholic? Self-sabotage. And yet, sex and success are two of the most heavily marketed themes in the western world! There is a reason for that truth.

Another form of self-sabotage is inventing obstacles to stay stuck. This type of Behavior can be impossible to spot because we are too busy blaming the world for our problems. The antagonist is never the person in the mirror. It's a heartbreaking dynamic.

Over the years, I have met people whose impact could be well beyond their wildest dreams. It's always humbling to stand in their presence. Sadly, in their mind, life is against them! Everything has to be put on hold until the magical world of "one day" appears. The hard cold truth is that "one day" never arrives because it's an avoidance mechanism. By embracing the person in the mirror, we live in the moment and all that affords.

Avoid less.
Protect the wind.

My mom was fifty-three when she was diagnosed with Stage 4 lung cancer. I was twenty-seven at the time. I was just beginning to rise above my troubled childhood when the diagnosis blew me out of the water. My progress came to an abrupt halt.

On the one hand was the woman who was sober by day and ever so kind to everyone she met. I never doubted her goodness as a human being. On the other hand was the alcoholic that believed people with certain license plates were out to get her. It's called wet brain, and it's a nightmare. Then there was the role she played in my traumatic childhood. How to reconcile the polarity? After her diagnosis, I would sit near her as she slept. Watching her breathe was reassuring yet wrought with despair. The gift of breath was evidence of life. Please, keep breathing, mom!

We had an incredible year together before her final trip to the hospital. As she collapsed in our living room, the sheer terror in her eyes was unmistakable. My response, worthy of a First Responder, calmed her until the paramedics transported her to the hospital. She fell in and out of a coma for several days, then suddenly sat tall in her bed. Her eyes were kind, at peace. "I love you," she said, lucid as though she never had cancer or morphine. After surveying the people in the room, she fell back into a coma. Moments later, she passed as I held her hand.

I was twenty-eight years old.
Everything went blank.
My world ended.

Tragedy and trauma take the wind out of our sails like few experiences in life. Any words I offer will fall short if such an event is fresh. Patience. Community. And a steady diet of feeling the feels got me through the despair. Even so, after my mom passed, the wind went silent for several years. It did return. It always does when we do the work.

Keep fighting.
Protect the wind.

Narcissistic individuals who battle intense insecurity know no bounds. Such individuals trigger easily and often, which makes them problematic when it comes to Black Sheep. Our very nature is seen as a threat. Typically, we are horrible at kissing ass. It's not our way. Some of us can strike a balance. That is an admirable quality. I am not one of those people! Avoid the elephant? I've already given it a pet name! But what if this person is a parent, sibling, spouse, or someone in a position of power?

Toxic behavior can take the wind out of your sails in an instant! Is staying silent worth the price? Independence is never free. Walking our path requires protecting our path.

Maintain strong boundaries.
Protect the wind.

Wind ignored is time thrown away! I have covered but a few wind killers. There are others. The more adept you are at protecting the wind, the more time you'll spend sailing the Seven Seas. Argh, me hearties, a Black Sheep life for me! The pirate vibe is rocking my world.

DEEP ROOTS & FULL SAILS

The disciplines of Oneness, Presence, and Sustenance keep you rooted in a soul-led life no matter the strife of a given moment. The roots remain! I cannot overstate the impact these disciplines have had on my life. Nor can I overstate my total disregard for them during the first thirty years of my existence.

Oneness anchors a deep sense of reverence for the gift of life. Presence ensures we don't miss anything along the way. Sustenance keeps us healthy during the ride. Our life is as sturdy as the rituals that anchor our existence. Under full sail, we are capable of incredible things. All we need is a compelling reason, an obsession or passion, anything that inspires us to act. Better yet, anything that inspires us to *consistently* take action. Always have persuasive reasons to persist.

Without the wind, we never begin.
Hoist the sails!

Everyone loses their way now and then. Find a reason to reignite your soul-led life. Lean into the three disciplines. Reclaim the wind that keeps you on the path.

THE VOICE WITHIN

How to find our reason for being? So much clutters the mind. Attempt to impress? We're all just doing our best! But inside, where there's no place to hide, we know the deal. We know what's real. Either something resonates as true to our core being, or it fails to meet that standard. The more present we are with ourselves, the easier it is to make that determination.

No matter how chaotic life gets, we can be ever mindful of our place in the world. *Our walk is a sacred walk.* That's not woo-woo bullshit! You can take it to the bank. Being fully present with our pain allows us to heal our wounds. Being fully present with our joy brings more joy into our lives. Being fully present with our bodies allows us to stay healthy and vital. There will always be chaos. That's a given. But when we treasure the moments, each moment has value.

Life is a gift.
Walk with reverence.

The first love note in this book is for my beloved Grams. She was one of a kind! Every few months, she would mail me a letter that always included a Garfield cartoon she clipped from her local newspaper. We could talk about anything. She was my rock.

I will never forget our phone conversation after she moved into an assisted living facility. It was the final chapter of her story. The weight of that truth sparked intense fear, but then she perked up. Grams had made it her mission to help newcomers when they first arrived. She overcame her fears by providing comfort to others. Even in the end, she owned her power. In purpose, she found peace. Grams passed away in her nineties, serving others.

A brief funeral service was scheduled in Arizona, but I was not invited. Her surviving children had already said their goodbyes. The funeral was nothing more than a formality. The whole thing felt wrong on many levels!

What is the value of an ordinary person who lived from a place of love? She was not wealthy or famous. And yet, the wisdom she shared shines brightly to this day. Her life mattered. It was a life worthy of celebration. I could not let this stand.

I asked a dear friend, a retired minister with a ton of Black Sheep edge if he would do a funeral service here in Austin? Of course, he replied. The memorial was held simultaneous to the one in Arizona. About twenty friends showed up, gifting flowers in memory of my beloved grandmother. It was a heartfelt celebration of her life. When the service was over, a small group of us gathered up the flower arrangements and got on a friend's boat. As we crashed through the waves of Lake Travis, I sprinkled flower petals on the water in tribute. I miss my four-foot-eight Grams.

Did a divine power call on me to act? I don't have a clue! Regardless, I am at peace with her passing. The actions of my uncles were callous and profoundly hurtful. But I had options if I kept an open mind. When my soul spoke, I listened.

Keep an eye on your compass.
Is it pointed True North?

In the film Forrest Gump, there is a scene where Forrest snaps. None of this is implicitly stated. Forrest just takes off running! At first, he runs to the end of the road, but his True North inspires him to keep moving. After traveling over 15,000 miles, Forrest finally put an end to his three-year sabbatical on sneakers. Apparently, he had a few things to work out. I can relate! Right?

When our soul has thoughts to share, it has a way of getting our attention. Connect with the things that are true to your core. Sometimes that takes a day. Other times, it takes 15,000 miles. It takes what it takes.

BUILD YOUR COMPASS

How to live a soul-led life? A Native American proverb offers much wisdom if we are willing to heed the call.

"Listen to the wind, it talks. Listen to the silence, it speaks. Listen to your heart, it knows."

Did you listen to the right voices? Make the right choices? It's hard to believe in things not visible to the naked eye. It's hard to have faith that you're headed the right way. But when something feels real and true, there are things to do. Trails to blaze. Don't get lost in the haze! Rush less. Hear more. Sail your own ship.

In the assignments that follow, you will build your Black Sheep Compass. While taking these exercises seriously is essential, don't let them weigh you down. Our work should be empowering, not cumbersome.

ESSAY#1: FIND TRUE NORTH

How to trust something within yourself if you're always looking out a window? It doesn't work! When you sit in silence, what do you hear? Describe the compass only your soul can see! What do you know? What do you believe? Finding True North is an inner journey. It requires exploring profound truths that already exist. It is a reverent, at times, maddening experience. Stick with the process. Do the work.

What do you *absolutely know* is *profoundly true* about yourself? That's the central question we will delve into in the following assignments. Absolute knowledge and profound truth speak to a very high level of certainty on your behalf. Please keep that in mind as you work through the various exercises. If negative thoughts pop up, ignore them for now. We'll take on a few topics to get started. When done, feel free to do some additional exploring if so inclined.

What informs your life?
Hear the wind!

Assignment #1 / What do you absolutely know is profoundly true about yourself as a human being? I'm an intense, playful, creative, geeky, a little wild, a little wise, principle-driven, hot mess of a super effective (albeit always daydreaming) human being. And that's just the appetizer round! What about you? Go bone marrow deep! Get to the real stuff, and jot down a few notes.

Assignment #2 / What do you absolutely know is profoundly true about yourself as a Black Sheep owner, artist, activist, whatever it is you do? Professionally speaking, what turns you on? What turns you off? How does your work or craft stand out in a crowd? Document your version of loud. Which has zero to do with hype and everything to do with the core passions that drive you professionally. Etch an authentic snapshot. Dig deep, then jot down a few notes.

Assignment #3 / What do you absolutely know is profoundly true about yourself as a creative or artist? Hummingbirds average 3,180 wing flaps per minute. That's my brain when in a hyper-artistic state, such as when I wrote this book or produced Breaking Beckett. I disappear into the inner world of my imagination. When I'm in a peak creative zone, I forget my keys, gas, food, showers, shaving, water, you name it. What about you? Pop open your brain! Tickle your artistic lobe, and jot down a few notes.

Assignment #4 / What do you absolutely know is profoundly true about yourself as a life partner? What about as a parent or friend? No risk, no reward! This particular assignment can be triggering. You're not doing a personal inventory. Nor or you rehashing old wounds or bad blood. Remain on solid, judgment-free ground. Zero in on the things that inform you when in a given role, such as lover, partner, parent, or friend. Bring down the walls. Connect with the relationships that anchor your life, and jot down a few notes.

If you would like to explore a few more areas to lock down your True North, please do so. As an aside, do not weaponize these assignments! Our work should be empowering, not shaming.

ESSAY #2: FIND YOUR IKIGAI

One of my favorite definitions of ikigai describes it as your reason for getting up in the morning. Another describes it as the things that make life worth living. Be careful with that last one. Tacos definitely make life worth living, but they are not a part of my ikigai! Or are they? Hmmm.

What brings *tremendous meaning* to your life? Focus on the modifier "tremendous" as you work through this set of exercises. My work as an amateur director was very gratifying, but bringing an artistic vision to life was the activity that brought tremendous meaning to my existence. Business success felt good, but making big things happen was the juice that fed my reason for being. I'm oversimplifying, but you get the point.

Lots of things feel good.
Very few feed your soul.

Assignment #1 / What brings tremendous meaning to your personal life? Jot down a few notes. What about your professional, creative, social, philanthropic, and spiritual lives? Take each area one at a time, and jot down a few notes. As a gentle reminder, you're not trying to flesh out pursuits that feel good. Instead, you're identifying the experiences that speak to you on a deep level. As a result, this will be a much smaller list than our True North work due to the narrow focus of this exercise.

Assignment #2 / Once you have fleshed out what brings tremendous meaning to your life, take a long look at your list. Of the endeavors you noted, which ones are also *central* to your reason for being? Please don't rush past the significance of this question! While various experiences have brought tremendous meaning to my life, very few are central to my reason for being.

I have dedicated much of my adult life to helping people. It is a core element of my ikigai. But the many ways I manifest that impact are not why I get up in the morning. While mentoring and teaching are fulfilling, they are not, in and of themselves, central to my reason for being. Making a difference anchors my reason for being.

Handcrafting the written word has been a part of my life for over forty years! But it's never been about the words. It's always been about the purpose those words serve, depending upon the context. This is true of any creative endeavor I take on. In many ways, I don't view myself as a writer in a traditional sense. My bad! Right? You already bought the book! But it's true.

Obedience to an established writing structure or winning awards based on those norms will never fuel my fire. I have no aspirations to become the supreme leader of a writer's commune. My creative work always serves a broader purpose. Hooking into that purpose on an ongoing basis is how I manifest my ikigai.

Clarify your reason for being, but keep it simple. It's easy to do a ton of work without ever making progress. Plant a few seeds, then see where they go. Don't overthink it.

Hit pause. Before diving into your final assignment, take a long, indulgent break. Ideally, a few days or more to process your work. Let it marinate beneath the surface.

ESSAY #3: ASSEMBLE YOUR COMPASS

Assignment #1 / Your True North informs your life. Your Ikigai gives it purpose and meaning. Your Black Sheep Avatar doubles down on your authentic self. Combine the three into a single document titled "My Black Sheep Compass." If so inclined, add graphics, art, music, or anything else that brings your compass to life.

While this assignment may feel abstract on paper, it can be life-altering upon completion. Think about it for a moment. Everything that defines you as a human being can be found in a single document. Your deepest truths are brought to life to guide your life. What's the alternative? It's hard to feed a soul we've never met.

CONTEMPLATIVE JOURNALING

Feed Your Soul

The life-defining choice to feed your soul is a choice to live a soul-led life. Rush less. Hear more. Stay centered. Protect the wind. Use your compass. The Secret Sauce to living a life of purpose and meaning.

1) Create a title page. Write Life Choice #4, and then a few spaces below, write, Feed Your Soul. Dress up the page with graphics if that's your thing. Make this contemplative session your own!

2) Add a few pages of actionable insights from this chapter. An insight is actionable when it moves you to act in a specific way. Throughout this chapter, we explore living a soul-led life. If I were reading versus writing this book, I would flesh out how to do that on a daily basis. Look for insights that inspire you to act!

HABIT #1: LIVE WITH INTENTION

Unplug. Clear your mind. Be fully present. Forge authentic connections. Live in your body. Live in your truth. Proceed with purpose, and persist with passion.

Expand Your Self-Awareness / Elevating your self-awareness directly impacts your ability to influence the outcomes of your life. Developing a meditation practice, taking mindfulness classes, and practicing yoga are a few options. Find an approach that resonates.

Stay awake.
Exist in the present tense.

Grow Deep Roots / We sustain our connection with a soul-led life by actively practicing the three disciplines of Oneness, Presence, and Sustenance. How will you make this happen? What's the plan? Begin your practice!

Find your center.
Anchor your existence.

Stay In The Zone / Absent purpose, passion, and a clear direction, we stagnate. How will you keep your sails full? How will you protect the wind? List a few action items that resonate from our work in this chapter.

Stuck has a solution.
Keep your sails full!

3) Set aside twenty pages to work on the first habit. Use the first page of this habit as the title page. Write, "Feed

Your Soul: Habit #1 - Live With Intention." Add graphics and visuals if that's your thing. Make it your own!

4) How to get better at living with intention? What resources do you need? What action steps need to happen? Make it real. Be specific. Develop a new habit. As a reminder, Rome was not built in a day. Be gentle with yourself! Progress, not perfection.

HABIT #2: USE YOUR COMPASS

Live, build, and create from a well that runs deep! Your compass connects you to the water that feeds your soul. Are you drinking enough water? Stay hydrated! Where to begin? Here are a few ideas to help you get started!

Show Your Skin / Use your Black Sheep Avatar to own the edge that gives you an edge. List tangible ways to showcase the epic value you bring to the world. Find your version of Black Sheep bold! Make a statement! How to showcase your persona in a way that resonates?

Speak your truth.
Walk in your power.

Travel True North / How can you integrate your True North work with your daily routines to bring your life into alignment? When True North becomes a tangible tool, life becomes a richer, more purposeful experience.

Listen with intention.
Act with intention.

Honor Your Ikigai / Blasting past the things that infuse your life with meaning leads to autopilot. Slow down! How can you connect with your reason for being? How will you sustain that connection?

Rush less.
Connect more.

5) Set aside twenty pages to work on the second habit. Use the first page of this habit as the title page. Write, "Feed Your Soul: Habit #2 - Use Your Compass." Add graphics and visuals if that's your thing.

6) How can you get better at using your Black Sheep Compass? What resources do you need? What action steps need to happen? Make it real. Be specific. Develop a new habit. As a reminder, Rome was not built in a day. Be gentle with yourself! Progress, not perfection.

7) Celebrate! It's not easy to do this kind of work, but it is worthwhile. You are investing in yourself! You are

learning to own your Black Sheep voice and powers. Do something nice for yourself. Get in the habit of celebrating your victories, large and small.

True North is found using a compass only your soul can see. Walk barefoot in silence. Twirl in the pouring rain. Play with childlike glee. Surrender to a long embrace. Be less than perfect. Ask for help. Lend a hand. Chase a dream. Do your thing. Apologize. Then realize True North rarely screams. It's just something you know when the pace is slow.

Feed your soul!

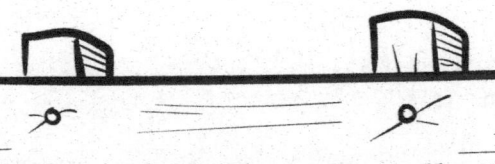

Greetings, Black Sheep Traveller!

I hope this book speaks to you personally and you discover tangible tools along the way! **If this rogue literary experience hits home, please review it on Amazon.** A flood of Amazon love that speaks to this book's impact helps me get the word out. In an ideal world, this rebel tome will become a must-read manifesto for our eclectic tribe of Black Sheep thinkers and creators.

I appreciate your support,

Bobby Ford

CHAPTER #6

MEET THE MOMENT

"Luck is what happens when preparation meets opportunity."

Stoic Philosopher Seneca

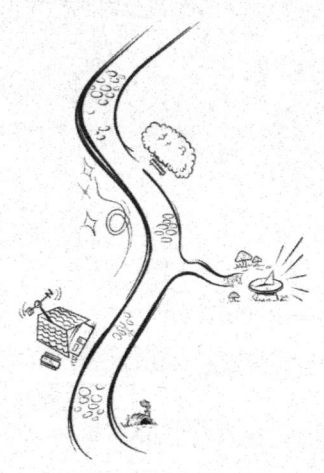

Opportunity knocks! Concealed or fully revealed, the moment arrives. Your anxiety soars in disbelief, then finds relief in potential made real. You're standing at a crossroads. Which way to go? How to proceed? It's the eternal battle of want versus need.

Neurons explode left and right. Gears turn. Ideas churn. Endless options blast through your brain. A tidal wave of thoughts floods the page. Settle in. Grab a cup of tea. If it's meant to be, and all that poppycock! It's wisdom that never works. Ok, so occasionally, it works. Still, the question remains. What to do in this pivotal moment? Don't throw away your shot!

Slow your heartbeat. Close your eyes. Refuse to compromise. Look for the answers in your soul-led life! Slowly, patiently, after plenty of steps, you get the sense that destiny awaits. Your story is being written before your very eyes. A few minutes pass, then hours. A long pause steals the air. The world disappears. It's time to decide. Play it safe, or open a new door?

Ease the pace. Exit the race. Spot the intersection that could alter your life. Choose your path. Decide your fate. No guarantees! Fail or succeed. Opportunity knocks.

ORDINARY EXTRAORDINARY HUMANS

The bread and butter of Black Sheep bold is our ability to see the world through a different pair of glasses. We need to *trust our value* to wield our mystical might. Not blindly! That would be reckless. Trust is earned.

Do I have what it takes? Is my talent up for the task at hand? Roam uncharted land! In the act of doing, we clarify our value. Tiny steps taken slowly awaken our most potent abilities. Step, stumble, and succeed. That's the formula! Rinse and repeat. Take detailed notes. Make adjustments along the way.

Meeting the moment is being ready to rock long before the moment ever arrives. It's the key that opens the treasure chest. Opportunity knocks. Play your best hand. Messy is a given. Meet the demand. It's how ordinary people do extraordinary things.

> *Preparation is key.*
> *Fertilize the soil!*

Extraordinary happens when a mortal is properly prepared and willing to act. Inherent within this truth is the willingness to fail, which happens often. It's all a part of the process. Are you prepared to fail? It's a serious question. We avoid danger because who wants to crash and burn? Hell, I don't want to crash and burn! But fail, we must. Repeatedly. Ouch! It sucks. Here's the thing. The people who bring tremendous value to their work or craft know failure well. There is always a price to pay.

ESSAY #1: ELEVATE YOUR EXPERTISE

I landed my first sales job in my mid-twenties. It was a big deal. It felt like a miracle, given my upbringing. How to succeed in a career that offers a way out? It was an overwhelming yet exhilarating opportunity. There was no plan. I was hungry, for what, who knows?

Several nights a week, I parked my company car, a red Ford Tempo, in a wealthy neighborhood that overlooked the ocean. All the mansions had a golden glow that I find enchanting to this day. Once the interior car light clicked on, my study session commenced. Books, training tapes, and piles of scribbled notes installed the fundamentals of business. How to dress, talk, sell, time management and other topics set the stage for later success. Did I know this at the time? Not even a little bit! Still, my mobile university was a refuge. In the world of knowledge, I walked with great minds.

Eventually, I grew out of my seaside studies. Cal State Long Beach dedicated an entire floor of its library to business. Imagine the possibilities! I studied marketing, branding, TQM, servant leadership, and the mechanics of peak performance. Cramming Peter Senge's, *The Fifth Discipline*, a deep dive on systems thinking, laid the foundation for my eventual consulting practice. Being a pretend undergrad had its perks!

Why study in a car? Why pretend to be a college student? My business career was not the byproduct of a supportive family (which did not exist) nor an articulated plan. The disastrous date happened just a few years before this era of my life. My mother's alcoholism was so bad she could no longer function. Pursuing a traditional education was not in the cards. I did what I had to do to succeed. It's a lonely memory thick with despair. But it's also a point of pride. I am a proud graduate of Red Ford Tempo University! No, we don't have a football team.

Avoid excuses.
Find a way.

My origin story is less about my feral approach to self-education than the mentality it embedded. Immersing myself in a field of study opened doors once thought off-limits. Knowledge leveled the playing field. My thirst for insight and ideas remains as insatiable as ever. I cannot overstate the need to keep your mind ravenous.

Decades later, immersing myself in studies happens without thought. It's in my DNA at this point. As mentioned in the dedication, Hamilton became the internal metronome for this book. According to iTunes, I've listened to the soundtrack five times and various songs over sixty times! Work! Whatever the passion, saturating my brain levels the playing field.

Stack the deck.
Feed your mind.

ESSAY #2: EXCEL AT YOUR CRAFT

What fundamental skill sets earn you a seat at the table in your industry or wherever you do your thing? You may choose to adapt, elevate, or even transform those core skill sets, but starting out, you need to establish a rock-solid foundation. How will you make the most of an opportunity if you don't understand the fundamentals that drive your space? People won't take you seriously. You need to know your stuff. The prerequisite to disruption is mastery.

A Black Sheep activist, social entrepreneur, artist, restauranteur, fill in the blank, works hard to excel at every aspect of their core craft. It is in the pursuit of mastery that we spot potential. In plowing the soil, we get a better feel for our capabilities. In honing our process, we level up our talent and impact. Hacks are of little use. It takes what it takes. Put in the time. Pay your dues. When your work or craft rises above the crowd, hit pause. Take a closer look. What got people talking? Be specific. How might you use these insights going forward? Success leaves clues. Follow the clues. Identify your Secret Sauce. Learn the recipe.

Doing our thing is rarely the grandiose version that lives in our heads. To be super clear, dream big! Have a blast! I have done countless interviews with Oprah in my magical mind. Such daydreams add fuel to the fire. Meanwhile, back on planet earth, I probably need to excel at the fundamentals before Oprah sends me an invite. As we elevate our impact and visibility, we get ever closer to the mountain we seek to claim.

Walk the path.
Perfect your craft.

The painful lessons that preceded this book were a necessary part of the process. Am I happy that was the case? Would you be happy after running naked through a hundred miles of cactus? I don't think so! That was the price of admission. Opportunity requires payment in full. There is no installment plan.

ESSAY #3: TRUST YOUR HUNGER

Imagine participating in the pitch for Ka, one of Cirque du Soleil's shows in Las Vegas. It's hard to comprehend.

"Hear me out! I'm about to blow your mind! The show will have two main platforms. One of them will be five stories tall, half that in width, and weigh fifty tons. Despite its gargantuan size, we'll be able to rotate the stage into multiple positions. Did I mention the platform looks like it's floating in thin air? Crazy, right? But it gets better! Defying the laws of physics, the final battle will be fought vertically. That's a ten-story drop from the top of the stage to the bottom of the pit! Who's with me?"

Have you lost your damn mind? That would have been my response. I'm all about taking risks, but that would have been a bridge too far! To say Ka is breathtaking does not come close. As I said, opportunity requires payment in full. Robert Lepage spent twenty-five years honing his craft in theater and film before he became the creator of Ka. True, most of us will never create something on that scale. Still, the need to push the envelope burns beneath the surface. As Black Sheep, we are driven by intense passions that can be hard to comprehend.

Extraordinary is born of hunger.
What feeds your hunger?

She is twenty-six years old. We have only spoken on the phone once, and as of this writing, we have never met in person. Her smokey vocals peak where heaven begins, then drop low into your soul. She's the surgeon, and you're her patient. Helpless, you surrender to the medicine that is her music. Her name is Adiana Vega. She's a musician on Twitch, a streaming platform, but that doesn't even begin to scratch the surface!

The impact of COVID. The stress and strain. Racial violence. Racial pain. Adi has real conversations with her online tribe. After the Uvalde massacre, her tears gave voice to our grief, and her words gave voice to our outrage. Soulful music. Vulnerable fellowship. You are seen in her eclectic world. People share. People care.

Milady Vega was brand new to Twitch when I joined her community. At the time, the stream had maybe fifty followers. Twenty months later, it has over five thousand! She has raised thousands of dollars for charities. Adiana's community recorded over eight hours of video for her first anniversary as a streamer to express their love and gratitude. Think about all the lives she has touched in just under two years.

Creating the next Ka is not what extraordinary looks like for many Black Sheep. Perhaps, that's the trap? We hold ourselves to impossible standards. Why even try? It's not about fame and fortune for many of us. It's about doing what we love to have the impact we crave.

Claim your version of extraordinary.
What might that look like?

THE CROSSROADS

When we miss the knock at the door, the door remains closed. The opportunity, its potential, is never exposed. Will it be the spark that got away? It's hard to say when looking back in time. Granted, plenty of road remains.

Pivotal: of crucial importance in relation to the
development or success of something else.

The problem is the fork in the road we missed. What was the impact on our lives? Ease the pace! Open your eyes. Miss fewer moments. Bravely doing our thing depends on our ability to navigate the pivotal crossroads of life.

Crossroads: a turning point or opportunity
to change course, direction, or goal.

How to proceed when in a bind? There's no escaping the events that brought you to this place and time. Something feels off. That's all you know. Which way to go? The optimal route is rarely clear. Flying by the seat of your pants never works. It often worsens the situation. How to end a toxic cycle of staying stuck? How to break free from a prison of your own making?

ESSAY #1: SEVEN PIVOTAL MOMENTS

#1 / A physical crossroads moment is when your body turns on itself. All is not well! Symptoms get worse. An impromptu visit to an emergency room becomes a wake-up call. Your body starts to crash. Or maybe you're just tired of feeling like crap. Whatever the trigger, it's time to start taking better care of yourself. What's the plan?

#2 / A personal crossroads moment is when you hit a wall. Life has lost its luster! Facing an addiction. Grieving the loss of a loved one. Developing good financial habits. Dealing with the emotional toll of COVID. Whatever the trial, life as you knew it has left the building! Find your way back home. How will you make that happen?

#3/ A professional crossroads moment is when the status quo sucks your soul dry. Maybe it's time to explore your options? An opportunity appears that cannot be ignored. Your industry is no longer a good fit. It's time to open your studio. Here's the problem. Competing interests can muddy the waters. Your need to make money may be at odds with your desire for change. What's the solution?

#4 / A creative crossroads moment is when The Fire Within fades to black! The passion that once fueled your craft becomes an obligation to pay the bills. Creating, performing, writing, designing, whatever it is that you do, it's getting harder by the day. Have you lost your mojo? It's a terrifying question. What if it never comes back? Treading water is no longer an option. Are you burnt out? Do you need an extended period of renewal? Or is it time for a wholesale change? Find your fire!

#5 / A spiritual crossroads moment is when you have a crisis of faith. What's the point of it all? Life lacks meaning. Your soulful center is adrift. Feeling untethered from the world can be very isolating. A spiritual fracture may or may not have to do with religion. An agnostic can experience such a dilemma no different than a religious person. How to reconnect with your soulful center in a way that is authentic to your beliefs?

#6 / An organizational crossroads moment is when your ship veers off course. Hard right rudder! Your once stout brand starts taking on water. COVID destroys your revenue base. A new board chair drives your non-profit into the ground. Your startup's rapid success turns into financial stress. No matter the storm, you need to steady the ship. How will you get that done?

#7 / A societal crossroads moment is when a major event shatters our daily lives. What the hell is happening? I don't know what to do! The massive repercussions of the pandemic. Russia's unjust invasion of Ukraine. The January 6th insurrection in the United States. How to cope when the world turns upside down?

My mantra for decades was, "Ride life hard and go out screaming!" I used those exact words! Oh, Bobby, of years past. Sigh. You missed a few crucial crossroads along the way, Bubba. Everyone does, even the dude that wrote this book. Progress, not perfection. Still, debunking that closely held mantra was no easy task.

Work hard. Play hard. It was crazy levels of toxic. People can balance the two just fine. I am not one of those people! The person in the mirror had become a stranger until I stopped riding life hard. Until we wake up, we stay numb. Hard truths? Epic opportunities? I missed those moments until my authentic self came back online at age thirty-nine. To spot the pivotal crossroads of life, we must break through the fog.

The things we ignore, we store.
Remember that one?

Close your eyes. Take a deep breath. Hold it for a few seconds, then exhale from a *place of presence*. Repeat the ritual until you find your center. Hold space for the assignment that follows.

Assignment #1 / Grab a notepad, laptop, or whatever you prefer. When have you successfully navigated a physical challenge that was pivotal to your life at the time? Briefly describe the event. What helped you effectively navigate that tricky intersection? Please be specific. Finally, how did meeting that moment positively impact your life? Again, please be specific.

Once you're done noodling the first pivotal moment, work through the next six moments from the list, one at a time. If you struggle to find examples of meeting the moment, know they exist. Seek outside support if need be to finish the assignment.

Elevating your ability to spot pivotal moments keeps you in the driver's seat. Life is unpredictable. Your response to it can be purposeful. No one spots all of the intersections, nor would that be healthy. Strike a balance between seeing with all of your senses and the escapism that keeps you on solid ground. Fun is good for the soul! Tuning out. Naughty time. Getting your mind off the stress and strain. Strong medicine as long as you don't lose your sense of self.

LIGHTNING IN A BOTTLE

The grand vision you seek is unlikely. Rarer than a miracle. Perhaps, for a lucky few, but not you. Get your head out of the clouds! Get back to work! Listening to your heart is foolish. Wait in line for your time. Tick-tock. Wait in line for your time. Tick-tock. Wait in ...

Well-intentioned or not, such advice is ludicrous. You can do almost anything with the right set of tools. When improbable roads converge, give in to the urge to meet the moment. As impossible as the journey may seem, stay the course. Be effective. Pursue your passions.

> *Our walk is a sacred walk.*
> *Trust the person in the mirror.*

If you have already accomplished a lot in your life, the opening for this section may feel rudimentary. You've been there, done that, and you got the t-shirt! I have given counsel to my share of millionaires. Guess what they all have in common? Everyone has hidden potential to unlock. Discover the lightning you have yet to unleash!

ESSAY #1: SURVEY THE LANDSCAPE

Initially, we discussed the importance of fertilizing the soil before pivotal moments arrive. Next, we elevate your ability to navigate those moments when they land at your doorstep. What to do with a bolt of lightning buzzing about in your Mason jar? You can't store it next to the pickles!

The initial premise of this book was rethinking our life's work. All my research was built around that initial premise. Early in chapter one, I created the Black Sheep Proud™ sectional title without the trademark. Instantly, glass shattered, and a lightning bolt struck! My book took off in a completely different direction in that pivotal moment. It came to life in ways far beyond my wildest dreams. The 100 foot wave reappears! And trust me, it felt like it. I could have ignored the lightning bolt from a place of fear. My original premise feels so comfy cozy, like a warm blanket on a cold winter's night.

Are you here with me, Bobby Ford?
Are you fully present?
Essential questions endure.

Interestingly, all the chapters, the book cover, and my artwork instructions, for the most part, remained intact. The Black Sheep Proud™ logo, my author website and business cards were created within a few weeks. My book found its purpose, and I found my voice as the author. Even so, serious problems remained. My writing was devoid of life. It was time to take a break.

I had fallen in love with Hamilton on Disney Plus when it first came out. Maybe that would resuscitate my writing? Halfway through the show, lightning struck again! Riffs exploded onto the page, one after another. When I circled back around for edits, one thing became clear. My book had become Dr. Seuss for adults. Too many riffs,

Bobby Ford! Green Eggs & Black Sheep Ham is not a thing. Danger, Will Robinson! Sigh. It took five months to write the first three chapters, of which only two made the final cut with minimal reworks. Opportunity requires payment in full. There is no installment plan.

On the surface, it sounds like this book is the result of a few pivotal moments. In reality, years of moments led to the lightning strike. Picture a domino line the size of a football stadium. Tipping the first one sets off a chain reaction. Given the scale, it takes time for the last domino to fall. When it does, fireworks light up the night sky. What do we notice? The fireworks!

The decision to seize the moment is kin to tipping the first domino. Fed up with being drunk all the time, you walk into an AA meeting to ask for help. What's next? Survey the landscape. After years of working for someone else, it's time to launch your socially conscious business. What's next? Survey the landscape. Starting a social revolution? Survey the landscape. You get the point. Tipping the first domino is just the beginning.

It's the dawn of a new day. A moment is met, and yet, the unknown awaits. Stop for a second. Get your bearings. Look around. You walk upon virgin ground. It won't go smoothly! It never does, nor should that be the goal. Once you meet the moment in earnest, the train leaves the station. Your decision takes on a life of its own. It's palpable. You can feel the shift.

All aboard!
The first domino falls.

ESSAY #2: CREATE A ROADMAP

Assignment #1 - What do you need to know? / As I have stated multiple times, knowledge is power. Meeting the moment requires a sober assessment of the situation at hand. Understanding the core mechanics of self-publishing paved the way for this rogue literary experience. Clarifying a path forward offers hope if you're working through an intense challenge. What knowledge do you need to navigate this pivotal moment in your life? Ponder the question, then jot down a few notes.

Assignment #2 - What do you need to test? / Testing is where the rubber meets the road. Once I decided to write this book, I told everyone with a pulse about my intentions. In so doing, not only did I double down on my decision, I got invaluable feedback. It's tough to put yourself out there when your vision is not entirely clear. It's a vulnerable yet essential part of the process. Take your soul-led elevator pitch out for a test drive! The only way to know if the water is too cold is to jump in the water. What, specifically, do you need to test? Ponder the question, then jot down a few notes.

Assignment #3 - What do you need to change? / Not too long ago, I hit a wall. Getting my book done was two months behind schedule. I stopped running three times a week. Hydrating fell through the cracks. Push through, Bobby Ford! Put the pedal to the metal! My body was collapsing under the stress. The thing I wanted, getting this book done, was at odds with my need to take good care of myself. What do you need to change to navigate this pivotal moment in your life? Ponder the question, then jot down a few notes.

Assignment #4 - What do you need to do? / A crucial component to being effective is understanding the difference between wants and needs. Launching a book has specific needs. It would be easy to ignore those core needs, wasting valuable resources to make myself feel good. I *needed* twelve pieces of artwork to elevate the reader's experience. I *wanted* twenty-plus works of art, which would have delayed the release and ramped up the cost. Grandiosity is not your friend. What needs to happen to navigate this pivotal moment in your life? Ponder the question, then jot down a few notes.

Recap / How to effectively seize the moment when blindfolded? It won't happen! You need a roadmap. Your effectiveness skyrockets when the path forward is clearly understood. Progress happens one meaningful step at a time. Your job? Tip the first domino! When the moment is right, the lightning will strike. When standing at a pivotal intersection of life, create a roadmap.

ESSAY #3: TAKE BOLD STEPS

In my mid-thirties, a former vendor reached out to discuss an opportunity with a boutique ad agency. The firm was experiencing growing pains. Perhaps it was time to jump into consulting? The mental picture of giving advice for a living was intoxicating. Lightning had struck! A game changer was pounding on my front door.

The day after my interview, I sent a pink gorilla to deliver a large bouquet of mylar balloons and a massive greeting card to the agency's owners. "It's a boy!" adorned each balloon. An ultrasound had revealed their new marketing consultant had been found. That was the message inside the card. Long story short, I got the job.

After my first month, another opportunity knocked on the door. While the agency was kicking ass, the struggles my former vendor had noted could not be ignored. Despite my brief tenure, I submitted a detailed Consultative Brief with hard-hitting recommendations. Soon after, I became the General Manager. At this point, I had only been with the firm for two months or so.

To be clear, the risks I took were informed and backed by years of credible expertise. We're back to the first section of this chapter, right? Fertilize the soil. Put another way, gimmicks don't open doors. Using a pink gorilla to tip the first domino? Sure, that can work in the right situation. Audacity serves a purpose. What's the goal?

The pink gorilla and consultative brief let loose a flurry of lightning bold. Each hit its intended target. No one saw it coming! It soared above the crowd. When standing at a crossroads, make your response unmistakable.

The value you offer is the sentence.
Audacity is the exclamation point.

Assignment #1 / Suing my parents for emancipation opened the door to every positive outcome that followed! Studying in my car helped me land my first big sales position. The pink gorilla fertilized the soil, which became my consulting practice for sixteen years. Three intense years in recovery taught me life skills that continue to serve my life. Connecting the dots builds confidence. Connecting the dots is proof positive that audacious action gets results.

Audit Your History. Identify a decision that altered the course of your career or craft in a good way. Dig deep! What led up to the big moment of truth? Describe the first domino to fall and the chain of events that followed. Why did you pick this particular crossroads memory? Fleshing out the connective tissue between a bold choice and its impact encourages more gutsy decisions.

Assignment #2 / The insights I offer have nothing to do with the cinematic version of audacity. Acts of courage rarely manifest in a manner that is bigger than life. It is in the quiet moments that we commonly make brave choices. That said, yes, there are times when the best solution is audacity. So, be it. Let the lightning strike!

Audit The Present Day. What do you need to stop tolerating? What are you avoiding? Let me ask that last one again because it's essential. *What are you avoiding?* It's all good. Avoidance is an issue for all of us. Where are you whispering when you need to go loud? What pivotal moments are you dealing with in the here and now? Swim in a pool of reality. It does wonders for the soul. How else to make progress? Jump in the deep end! Where do you need to be audacious? Every now and then, Black Sheep bold is the perfect response.

NOTE IN A BOTTLE

Elevating your expertise opens doors. Excelling at the fundamentals creates opportunity. Lightning strikes boost your impact and visibility. Such is the soil that meets the moment. Preparation plus opportunity equals luck. How to win the lottery? Fertilize the soil!

CONTEMPLATIVE JOURNALING
Meet The Moment

Tend to the soil. Elevate your impact. Get really good at lightning in all its forms. Tip dominos. When opportunity knocks, you'll be ready to answer the door.

1) Create a title page. Write Life Choice #5, and then a few spaces below, write, Meet The Moment. Dress up the page with graphics if that's your thing. Make this contemplative session your own!

2) Add a few pages of actionable insights from this chapter. If I were reading versus writing this chapter, I would zero in on getting better at spotting the pivotal moments. Look for insights that inspire you to act!

HABIT #1: FERTILIZE THE SOIL

We are the soil and seed. The things we manifest are the things we feed. Work the land of your mind! Good dirt delivers a bountiful harvest. Where to begin? Here are a few ideas to help you get started!

Core Training / What skill sets earn a seat at the table in your work or craft? Immerse yourself in a field of study. Work with a mentor. Create a roadmap for your growth. How will you scale your impact and visibility?

> *Excel at the fundamentals.*
> *Where to begin?*

Personal Development / Learn new things. Explore potential hobbies. Stay curious. Get help. Heal. Push yourself in healthy ways. Get out of your comfort zones. Target a few areas. Feed your mind!

> *Where do you need to grow?*
> *Fertilize the soil.*

Professional Development / The list of things we might break, create, invent, or transform is endless. What impact do you crave in the present tense? How will you set the wheels in motion?

Feed your fire!
Fertilize the soil.

3) Set aside twenty pages to work on the first habit. Use the first page of this habit as the title page. Write, "Meet The Moment: Habit #1 - Fertilize The Soil."Add graphics and visuals if that's your thing. Make it your own!

4) How to get better at fertilizing your soil? What resources do you need? What action steps need to happen? Make it real. Be specific. Develop a new habit. As a reminder, Rome was not built in a day.

HABIT #2: SEIZE THE MOMENT

Hidden behind secret doors, easy to ignore, are the most significant opportunities of your life. Crack the code. Unlock the treasure chest! Where to begin? Here are a few ideas to help you get started!

Spot More Moments / Doing the exercises will help. Improving your self-awareness, as covered in the previous chapter, is crucial. How will you grow your skill sets in this critical area? What's the plan?

Build your radar!
Opportunity knocks.

Process Your Options / You're standing at a crossroads What to do? Get a lay of the land. What do you need to know, test, change, and do? Consult your compass. Get good advice. Tend to new soil. Play the long game.

What's the plan?
Create your roadmap.

Rise To The Occasion / Stay out of your head. You have what it takes. Fight for the things that matter! Go Black Sheep bold. Don't let fear take hold. What bold steps get you in the game? What's your play?

Tip the first domino.
Make it memorable.

5) Set aside twenty pages to work on the second habit. Use the first page of this habit as the title page. Write, "Meet The Moment: Habit #2 - Seize The Moment."Add graphics and visuals if that's your thing.

6) How can you get better at seizing the moment? What resources do you need? What action steps need to happen? Make it real. Be specific. Develop a new habit. As a reminder, it is progress, not perfection.

7) Celebrate! It's not easy to do this kind of work, but it is worthwhile. You are investing in yourself! You are learning to own your Black Sheep voice and powers. Do something nice for yourself. Get in the habit of celebrating your victories, large and small.

Slowly, patiently, after plenty of steps, you get the sense that destiny awaits. Your story is being written before your very eyes! A few minutes pass, then hours. A long pause steals the air. The world disappears. It's time to decide. Play it safe, or open a new door?

Meet the moment!

CHAPTER #7

MAKE RAIN

"Ever tried. Ever failed. No matter. Try again. Fail again. Fail better."

Samuel Beckett

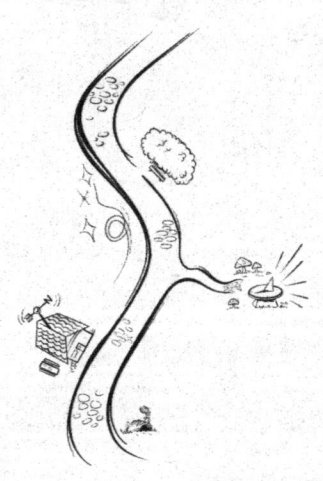

Doing big things. Realizing dreams. It's never as easy as it seems. Dig deep. Push hard. Don't let go. Resilience is the star of this show! Anything less than your soul-led best could fall short. The driving force has to be real, lest you run out of gas.

One person's normal may be your version of grand. It's relative to the situation at hand. Where are you in your story? What chapter are you about to write? Get clear. Press forward. Work your plan. Climb the mountain. Plant your flag. Big things happen when you dig deep.

Afraid you'll lose your way? Steal a moment. Relax. Breathe. Connect with bold ideas conceived. Your Black Sheep compass remains intact. It has your back. Act with purpose. Persist with passion. Patiently proceed. Solve the puzzle to bring your vision to life.

Manifesting the things you feel compelled to build or create is a rollercoaster beyond compare. It can leave you lifeless. Spent. Motionless. The price can be high. Hold space. Exit the race. Be boring. Crash hard. Give yourself plenty of time to rest. Unwind. Then back to the road to do your thing. Such is the Black Sheep version of Yin & Yang.

REBEL THINKERS & CREATORS

People who see the world through a different pair of glasses make history every day. In most cases, we will never know their names or even know they exist. Yet, there they are, pushing against the tide. Courageous art that shatters norms. Resolute activism that calls out injustice. Dreamy culinary experiences that bring people together. The art of meaningful impact is alive and well.

You could become the next Steven Spielberg, Cesar Chavez, or Amanda Gorman. It could happen, but it doesn't need to happen for your impact to matter. Your value as a Black Sheep thinker and creator stands alone. The look that fits best is the one you're wearing. Burn the costumes! Throw away the masks! It's a noble act. How will you have the impact you crave?

Yvon Chouinard, the founder of Patagonia, wrote a bohemian business book titled "Let my people go surfing." In it, he shares ten principles that have informed his life as a conscious capitalist. Those principles are not buzzwords casually thrown on a page. Yvon Chouinard's impact on our world is an *authentic manifestation* of his Black Sheep DNA.

So, what about that DNA? How do Black Sheep, legendary and otherwise, add value to the world? Four hallmark traits stand out in a crowd.

ESSAY #1: INDEPENDENCE

Driven by a felt cause. Unrelenting! Unable to pause. Dialed into the milestones that build or create. It's how we measure progress. When necessary, burn convention to the ground. Make waves. Blow up the status quo. Purpose demands passion. It's a tricky juggling act. Doing visionary work. Paying the price. Doing our thing. How to unleash our mystical might without losing our way as human beings? The tension between the two is never-ending.

Rumor has it we're radical. Ruthless. Full of ourselves. It's a common stereotype. While I have met my share of toxic rogues, it's not the norm. Being opinionated is not the same as being an asshole! It's acceptable, dare I say, *necessary* to have a strong point of view. Absent that intensity, it's tough to do your thing. How to blaze a trail if you're constantly worried about pissing people off? Black Sheep ruffle feathers. Not maliciously, but it is an essential part of the equation.

Speak your mind.
Be a good human.

As stated, our kind comes in many flavors. Ergo, autonomy has many looks depending upon the person. It's your choice to make. The version that matters most is the one that aligns with your compass. Even so, the need for independence, whatever that might look like, is absolute. Black Sheep, don't wait for approval! Facilitate. Empower. Collaborate. All critical habits to your success. Yet, those traits serve a broader vision. How to articulate that vision without a strong point of view?

Get everybody on the boat.
Sail True North!

Unfortunately, I've been a fiercely independent dude my entire life. Contradicting myself? Not all versions of independence are good for the soul. While autonomy is healthy, fierce independence is isolating. We need people. Community. Finding our tribe matters.

Grab your phone. Play some feel-good tunes. Ignite your lighter, and wave it like you're at a rock concert! Too much? Rolling your eyes? People who need people! Ok, back to our regularly scheduled programming.

Independence is a blessing and a curse. Strong opinions. The willingness to do what it takes to have the impact we crave. Calling out bullshit. Independently building or creating because that's how we deliver our best work. All good stuff! Refusing to take prudent counsel. Having all the answers. Pushing people away when we need them the most. Doing it all yourself. Being too proud to ask for help. Not the road to meaningful existence or success. It's a blind spot I work on daily.

Fight for your vision.
Be vulnerable along the way.

My fondest hope is our time together positively impacts your life. Part of that impact comes from the tangible tools and insights I provide. Hopefully, you'll also learn from my mistakes and draw inspiration from my imperfections. Transformation starts with transparency. Our walk is a sacred walk.

ESSAY #2: VISION

A spark triggers your brain! Potential? The next hit musical? A way to solve a big problem? Thoughts race through your head! Create a mixtape? Start a nonprofit? Launch an online community? A few weeks pass. Minimal progress. The spark slowly fades. Time marches on. Sparks come and go until one of the embers sticks to your soul. The first domino falls!

The seed that initially captures your imagination is but a wee ember. Barely more than a glimpse. Still, it's a place to begin. Let's revisit Yvon Chouinard's story. An avid rock climber and environmentalist notices his gear damaging the rock faces he loves to conquer. A wee spark floats into the night sky. To solve the problem, Yvon starts making rock-friendly climbing equipment. Eventually, his first business, along with other glints of inspiration, becomes Patagonia.

> *One ember can alter your life.*
> *One spark can change the world.*
> *Look for wee little glints of inspiration!*

When visionaries are sold as superheroes, ordinary folk retract into the shadows. Who am I to facilitate a fantastic brand, art, revolution, or solution? It's not the cloth from which I'm cut. Visionaries are not born with the gifts they possess. An Imagineer's toolkit has been built over many years. The ability to transform a glimpse into a viable vision is an *artisan craft*. Did Yvon Chouinard instantly know his tiny enterprise would become a billion-dollar brand? I seriously doubt it! Where to begin? Authentically manifest your Black Sheep DNA! You'll fail. You'll succeed. Your soul will bleed. And along the way, your toolkit grows one tool at a time. C'est la vie!

Ok, lovely term, "authentically manifest," but what the hell does that even mean? Yvon Chouinard is an avid rock climber and environmentalist. Rub the two together, sparks fly, then boom! I have a passion for writing and profound love for the Black Sheep of the world. What might happen if I rub the two together? Boom!

Stay curious.
Play with fire.

True North rumbles, no longer willing to hide. Embers stir but most fade away. Look for the spark that remains. Where might it go? Nobody knows. Explore virgin land. When the moment is right, lightning will strike.

ESSAY #3: LEADERSHIP

In my late twenties, I became a Regional Sales Manager for a prestigious aviation school. My region covered five states. I had never been on a plane! My next promotion, a few years later with the same firm, was to National Sales Manager. What fueled my rapid rise? Apparently, turning around poor-performing companies is a thing. Who knew? It's an intense specialty to master. High risk! High reward!

Leadership is in my blood. When all hell broke loose, I was the dude that brought calm to the storm. When doing the impossible was the only option, I was the miracle worker that got it done. I'm grateful for the experience. While the money was good, it never stopped feeling surreal. How did a terrified boy from the streets of Los Angeles grow to do such grand things? I can draw a direct line between the skills that helped me transcend my rough childhood and my turnaround skills. And let's not forget my time at Red Ford Tempo University. Exceptional leadership is about much more than skills. Who we are is how we lead.

There are many types of leaders.
What's your jam?

The concept to understand concerning Black Sheep leadership is it needs to serve a purpose greater than your personal needs or ego. What do you want to build, create, or offer? Why should people care? How will it bring meaning and value to the world? Will it rise above the noise? Rock climbing gear that is environmentally friendly met those criteria. It was a compelling retail position that served a greater purpose than its founder. Leadership gets stuff done. Leadership is the pragmatic side of visioning.

Banksy turned street art mainstream while using it to spotlight numerous social issues. While mind-bending talent and urban edge was the catalyst, sustaining public interest required savvy leadership. I'm guessing Banksy mastered both skill sets or hired exceptional leaders to lend a hand. Having a massive impact is one thing. Sustaining that impact over the long haul requires a different set of tools.

What skill sets do you bring to the table? What skill sets are missing? How can you add to your toolkit? Who do you need to hire to offset your blind spots? If you're not the solution; hire the solution.

ESSAY #4: RESILIENCE

Do you feel the concepts in this book are beyond your reach? If not, onward! If so, you're not alone. We all need fresh starts. We all need do-overs. Take as many as you need. Blazing new trails as an independent visionary does not happen overnight. No one instantly brings that level of intensity to their work or craft. Please, patiently proceed. Take one meaningful step at a time.

Disney Plus has an excellent documentary about ILM (Industrial Light & Magic), the visual effects house created for the first Star Wars film. Central to the ILM origin story is the first Star Wars film, "A New Hope." People struggled to understand the vision George Lucas was trying to put on the screen. Funding was a constant battle. The technical demands seemed unachievable. It was the 100 Foot wave on steroids! One particular observation Lucas made in the documentary is pitch-perfect for this chapter.

"You got to be persistent under
impossible conditions."

If you've been breaking the rules for more than a minute, you already know George is spot on. Chasing fame and fortune is not a sustainable approach. The only reason a sane person persists when facing impossible conditions is they have a damn good reason for doing so!

You fight for a visionary project when you're *heavily invested* in that project. Intellectually. Emotionally. Monetarily. Creatively. Whatever it takes, you are going to make it happen. You'll find a way. No doubt, it's a heavy load to carry. At times, the work or craft can be tedious. But what's the alternative? Playing it safe? Hard pass! Doing the work you love? Pour another round! La Vie Bohème!

Listen to your compass. If your path is sucking the life out of you, explore your options. Trying to move boulders you loathe is a colossal waste of your Black Sheep life! A rocket without fuel stays stuck on the launch pad.

Why do a thing?
Clarify your motivations.

Typically, we fail repeatedly before we find the rocket that soars. When we do, everything changes. What do you crave so intensely that you're willing to endure impossible conditions?

ESSAY #4: MAKE IT REAL

The Netflix show, Chef's Table is an anthology of master classes on becoming a maestro in your given field. Specific episodes strike a chord so profound that I have watched them over twenty times each! You've heard this story before, yes? Does the musical Hamilton ring a bell? Work! The last piece of advice Massimo Bottura gives in a New York Times article from 2016 is understated.

Simple. And yet, in just eight words, he offers you a gateway to doing visionary work or craft.

"Always keep a door open
to the unexpected."

That's it? Yup. Ok, so there is a hell of a lot more to it, but I'm trying to make a point. Had I not spent twenty-plus hours with Massimo via Netflix, there would be no reason to search for such an article in the first place. Rewatching his Chef's Table episode felt like sitting with a beloved mentor. Maestro! To be in the presence of greatness is life-altering.

Assignment #1 / Why do you think Maestro Bottura gave this advice? Why keep the door open to the unexpected? Jot down your thoughts. How might this principle apply to your life, work, and craft? Add to your notes.

Assignment #2 / Watch the Massimo Bottura episode from Chef's Table with a notepad and pen at the ready. Whenever you notice a mentality, behavior or action that stands out, hit pause, and jot down your thoughts.

Assignment #3 / Compare your notes from the previous two assignments. What jumps out at you? Document the big takeaways. Put your notes where you'll see them often. Revisit your observations weekly for a few months. Notice the impact this ritual has on your mindset.

We barely scratched the surface of what it means to be a Black Sheep thinker and creator. My suggestion? Fertilize the soil! Listen to podcasts. Read books. Take classes. Watch documentaries on the four traits covered in this section. Do whatever it takes until these tendencies *live within you* on a daily basis.

PLANT YOUR FLAG

Imagine the coolest dog you have ever known. Gorgeous. Playful. Smart. You can't get enough of this dog! Then it starts frantically chasing its own tail for weeks on end. That's us when we jump from one thing to the next! Jumping around seeds self-doubt. We need a few wins for our aspirations to feel worthwhile. It confirms we're on the right path.

Success builds confidence.
Are you getting buffed?

Early in his life, Mr. Chouinard was driven by his passion for rock climbing and the environment. Absent that clarity, his first business, most likely, Patagonia, never would have happened. Black Sheep can struggle with being impulsive. Is that true of all of us? Of course, not! But it's a critical blindspot to track lest you lose your way. How to do your thing if you're chasing your tail?

Assignment #1 / Planting your flag is claiming visionary real estate. What projects must get done? What type of lifestyle is central to your wellbeing? What social issues are you committed to over the long haul? What values are unwavering? Please do not confuse this with setting goals. Planting your flag is identifying and adhering to the *nonnegotiable priorities* that inform your life, work and craft. Claim your real estate!

Patiently Proceed / In the ten pages that follow are ten assignments. I do not recommend doing them one after the other. Don't lose your mind! We've already covered a lot of territory in this chapter. Relax. Grab a cocktail or cup of tea. Maybe snag some epic takeout. Fire up your favorite playlist. Push out the distractions. Sink into The Zone.

When you are ready, order À la carte. Pick a group of assignments that speak to your current situation. Dive in, and enjoy the ride. The book isn't going anywhere. Blowing yourself out of the water is not helpful. Take the time you need. It's not a race. Avoid speed runs. Do quality work.

ESSAY #1: PURPOSE & DIRECTION

Life takes a sudden turn. We evolve. Our priorities shift. Tremendous joy. Crushing blows. Change is a given. In sacrificing the comfort of today, we unlock the potential of tomorrow. Ticktock. Ticktock. We live on borrowed time.

As I knock on the door to sixty, my priorities are rapidly evolving. Less work. More fun. Travel. Memorable time with the people I love. Artistically, one social justice project in the spoken word space and a micro-budget feature are on my production slate. Christening the beach bum part of my life, hopefully in Hawaii, is on the menu. I have memories to grieve and even more to celebrate. And this book is just the beginning of the conversation! Who knows what's behind the next set of doors? A brief glimpse of how purpose and direction are manifesting these days.

Assignment #1 / What brings *purpose and direction* to your life in the present tense? Craft a single paragraph that resonates. Please do not confuse resonance with never-ending bliss! The grief work I mentioned has been intense but crucial. Keep at it until you have a concise snapshot.

> *Live in your body!*
> *What rings true?*

Assignment #2 / Let your work marinate for a few days, then revisit the assignment. Add a final coat of polish if needed. Once you're done, spend time processing your responses. What stands out? Were there any surprises? Did anything trigger you? If so, dig a little deeper in that area. Were you too hard on yourself? Be honest! What are the big takeaways from your work? Once you have processed your notes, write a brief Purpose & Direction Statement for your life in the present tense.

It's a simple assignment. On the surface, there's not much meat on the bone. In truth, clarifying your purpose and direction in the *present tense* anchors your focus. Where are you headed? Chart your course!

ESSAY #2: RELENTLESS RESOLVE

Business success meant I could beat the odds. Launching a company opened the door to autonomy. Consulting put me in the spotlight. I'm not sure when it happened, but the shackles of societal expectations fell to the ground. No longer a child of the streets, I was free.

12 Step and the performing arts melted decades of armor. Recovery taught me life skills. The arts helped me find my voice. A vulnerable, more authentic version of myself rose to the surface. Five years and a few plot twists later, I wrote this book.

Find your version of relentless.
Open more doors!

How often do we have it all figured out? Almost never! And yet, we know when something rings true or when it's not up for negotiation. It's how Star Wars got made, Patagonia soared, and Dr. King changed history. Unrelenting determination gets stuff done!

Assignment #1 / Watch several documentaries that feature the Black Sheep you most admire. Choose films that speak to you. Which moments stood out? How did people exhibit relentless determination? What quotes did you put on paper? What about those quotes struck a chord? Cite specific behavioral traits, scenarios and decisions to maximize this exercise.

Assignment #2 / Pick three instances where your relentless determination positively impacted your life. How did you act? What did you believe? What, specifically, brought you to that level of intensity? What were your motivations? By understanding ourselves, we identify traits that help us down the road.

As I reflect on almost six decades of living, one poignant truth comes into view. No matter the struggle, we are capable of damn near anything. If we dig in and fight for the things we care about, we create our own kind of magic in this life.

ESSAY #3: ARTFUL OBSESSION

Artful as in clever or skillful. It's the difference between using obsession as a driving force for good or falling victim to its destructive qualities. When a project is all-consuming, we unleash an intensity of purpose that elevates our capabilities. Used properly, that intensity can stack the deck in our favor. Many of the concepts we've covered are triggered by well-managed obsession.

A compelling vision kidnaps my mind. Held hostage by powers unseen, it's more than a dream. The project must get done. Why hold back? Why play it safe? Nothing is gained! Sorry for the stress. Apologies for the strain. Create, succeed, create, crash, then create again! Tis the path I have chosen. Tis the air I breathe.

Feed the hunger.
Do your thing.

Assignment #1 - Get Focused / How to become the CEO of a major brand while directing a film and learning how to surf big waves? It's not possible! You will drown. Am I being dramatic? Yes, but for a reason. Diluting your focus will sabotage your success. Can you have a day job or a side hustle? Sure, because they're not occupying every waking thought. The only way to *masterfully manage* an all-consuming obsession is to give it your undivided attention. Anything less undermines your results.

An obsession, in this context, is a lone passion project you commit to getting done. No matter what it takes, you'll find a way. It is the film, business, nonprofit, book, music album, food truck, whatever, that must happen. Failure is not an option! It could take a few months or several years. No matter, you're all in. Name and claim the obsession that will become (or is) the central driving force of your work or craft. Give your passion project a title and deadline. For example, publish a Black Sheep manifesto in 2022.

Assignment #2 - Clarify Your Motivation / The thought of writing a book sent me reeling. The pros and cons battled it out for five years before I finally pulled the trigger. One profound realization turned the tide. My life's work. Everything I have survived, experienced and learned had to serve a purpose. How else to make sense of it all? I decided to write the book I desperately needed when young, but it did not exist. Boom! Lightning struck! The first domino fell. The journey began once my motivation was clear.

Follow the heat.
Look for fire.

The decision to build or create something that stands out is not, in and of itself, enough to sustain an obsession. Why must your project get done despite the obstacles and naysayers? It's a heavy load to carry. The price can be high. Why pay the price? What's in it for you? Put it in writing.

Assignment #3 - Sell Your Vision / When you start telling the world about your passion project, the shit gets real. Without stakes, nothing shakes, and everything remains the same! Remember that from Chapter Two? The ability to sell your vision before you have figured it out is Black Sheep gold. It's a crucial skill.

In coming out, you step up. Public proclamations make it real, then close the deal. As in, sealing the deal with you! Tell your barista, neighbors, total strangers, family, and friends about your passion project. Sell your vision! Don't worry about your elevator pitch just yet. Better to see how everything lands.

You're not looking for approval. Authentic reactions are the data you seek. What lands? What confuses people? Polish and perfect your project, but don't let that slow you down. It's time to go public. Perfect timing does not exist. Track your progress. Hold yourself accountable.

FYI / Your passion project could be anything. Everybody is at a different place in their Black Sheep journey. Your version of all-consuming obsession is likely different than mine. Get passionate about your path. Double down on your project. At the end of the day, that's all that matters.

ESSAY #4: AUDACIOUS ACTION

How do you make the impossible probable? Initially, it's not always clear. Dare to open the doors that make you tremble! Crash. Soar. Stay hungry for more until you bring your vision to life.

The Mantra / Early in my business career and later in the arts, one question drove my strategies. How can I deliver maximum results in the least amount of time? It's a valuable query that becomes a mantra when it forces you to prioritize quality (maximum results) and effectiveness (least amount of time) side by side. When spending client money or my own, maximizing my return on investment has always been a top priority. Funding is a limited resource. I never want to sacrifice potential due to a lack of capital. Like any mantra, it is relative to the challenges at hand. Nonetheless, learning to prioritize quality with effectiveness is a game changer.

Assignment #1 - Create A Launch Plan / Zero in on your passion project. What will it take to *fully realize* your vision? What types of people and resources will be critical to getting it done? What's the timeline? What's the budget? Flesh out the details. Think outside the box while remaining pragmatic. How will you measure success? Get granular. Ambiguity muddies the waters, which hurts the end result.

Work your way through each question. Take detailed notes. Save important files. Do research, which may include immersing yourself in multiple fields of study. The goal is to craft a well-thought-out, kick-ass starting point. That's it! Plan your work, work your plan. It's an axiom that's been around forever. Let your work marinate for a few days. Polish as needed until you feel confident you're not flying blind.

Assignment #2 - Prepare For Lift Off / Initially, I focused on lining up the resources needed to write this rebel tome. Once the writing was well underway, the priority became locking down the branding, publishing, and marketing pieces to the puzzle. My prep work gave me confidence. While a great deal remained unclear, I had enough clarity to begin the journey.

Take a hard look at the plan you created in the previous assignment. What needs to get done? Who do you need on your team? Where might you find the best people for those roles? Explore your options. Sell your vision. What resources do you need for an epic launch? What are the deadlines? Keep your budget top of mind. Please work through these questions, jotting down your answers as you go. Add your completed work to your launch plan.

Assignment #3 - It's time to fly! / It's never about a single big moment. It's about many moments and how well those milestones are managed. If you are reasonably stable after launch, then you have succeeded. That's it! End of story! Your launch is when the adventure truly begins. Star Wars got made despite a flood of obstacles. Once it came out in theaters, it could have bombed. What prevented the explosion? A Black Sheep filmmaker named George Lucas, his obsession to get it done the right way, a kick-ass story, and all the incredible people attached to the project.

Do everything In your power to make history with your launch. Hold nothing back. Make a statement! If you don't make history, but your rocket is still airborne, that's also a success. What's next? It's a good question to continually ask yourself. What will be your top priorities post-launch? How will you sustain momentum? As a reminder, your launch could be releasing your first music album, starting a political action committee, or opening a B&B. It can be anything. One type of launch is not better or more badass than another.

Disclaimer / If you have never gone through such a process, overwhelm can become an issue. Remember that young boy who sued for emancipation? The same guy that struggled with intense anxiety? A younger me would have found this section intriguing but intimidating. Completing the assignments adds to your toolkit. In time, you'll get better at making big things happen.

Driven to fertilize the soil? You have options. Books, classes, meetups and online communities like The Happy Startup School will deepen your skill sets. Still, don't let fear, anxiety, or anything else delay your dreams! Grab the bull by the horns. The best time to bring your vision to life is right now. Guarantees don't exist. Risk is ever-present. Jump in the deep end!

EVOLUTION

Give your ideas room to roam. One could go all the way! Don't cleave to the island of today. Sure, it's knowable. It's dependable. But is that true? I don't think so! I get the fear. What if it all goes wrong? It will, and it won't. That's the rodeo. Still, your wisdom grows. Your toolkit continues to expand. New opportunities appear. No one is born a Black Sheep badass. Progress, not perfection.

Words alone cannot adequately describe how hard it was to write this book. Creatively, it required juggling multiple styles of writing simultaneously. The emotional intensity kicked my ass. I have never been so utterly exhausted, nor have I ever been so proud. The prize is relative to the price.

Here's the deal. I was not born to write this book! Whatever gifts I may or may not possess are no better or worse than your gifts. The same is true of anyone I've quoted in this rebel tome. Visionary projects happen because we make them happen. And we do these breathtaking things not as gods but as messy, imperfect mortals. Yet another theme throughout this book. Do you have what it takes to bring your vision to life? Absolutely! So, what's the delay? Go for it! The notion you have to be a specific type of person to do visionary work or craft is total bullshit. You hold the keys. Are you keen to open new doors?

Black Sheep thrive when they evolve. It seems rather obvious, right? But that's not the case. When we don't scale our impact and visibility, we stay stuck. Will you overcome those challenges? Are you willing to evolve?

CONTEMPLATIVE JOURNALING
Make Rain

Embers become sparks. Ideas become obsessions. Bring your passion projects to life. Make big things happen! Do your thing. Have the impact you crave.

1) Create a title page. Write Life Choice #6, and then a few spaces below, write, Make Rain. Dress up the page with graphics if that's your thing. Please make this contemplative session your own!

2) Add a few pages of actionable insights from this chapter. An insight is actionable when it moves you to act in a specific way. If I were reading versus writing this chapter, I would double down on all the assignments in the Plant Your Flag section to sustain my intensity level. Look for insights that inspire you to act!

HABIT #1: FEED YOUR OBSESSION

When your mind is on fire, you're on fire. That's the Secret Sauce to staying in a peak state of endless opportunities. How to ignite your brain on an ongoing basis? That's the million-dollar question. Where to begin? Here are a few ideas to help you get started!

Feed Your Imagination / Get on a steady diet of books, workshops, podcasts, documentaries, whatever floats your boat, to keep your imagination fully engaged. How to best feed the creative side of your brain?

Live in a world of wonder.
Explore the possibilities.

Create A Production Slate / What are you working on right now? What do you want to be working on over the next five years? Only book high-commitment projects. Jot down a few notes about each venture, and the year you will begin working on the project.

Make your visionary world real.
Commit to creation!

Bring People Along / A vision shared is a vision you take seriously. Hidden ambitions are easy to abandon. What passions fuel your Black Sheep journey? How can you build a community around those passions? Go public!

Start a tribe.
Seed a movement.

3) Set aside twenty pages to work on the first habit. Use the first page of this habit as the title page. Write, "Make

Rain: Habit #1 - Stay Obsessed." Add graphics and visuals if that's your thing. Make it your own!

4) How to get better at staying obsessed? What resources do you need? What action steps need to happen? Make it real. Be specific. Develop a new habit. As a reminder, Rome was not built in a day. Be gentle with yourself. Progress, not perfection.

HABIT #2: CONTINUALLY BUILD OR CREATE

Prolific Black Sheep are constantly thinking, imagining, tinkering, testing, building, and creating. It's a lifestyle that is wired into our DNA. How to be effective? Here are a few ideas to help you get started!

Tell The Story / When your venture has a gripping story to tell, you authentically connect with your audience. How did your passion project get started? What stole your heart? What has pushed you to the brink? Share your humanity! Why do this project?

Craft your brand story.
Share it from a place of purpose.

Work The Plan / Focused action that supports the big picture yields the best results. What are the top priorities? What tasks and deadlines support those priorities? What are the deliverables? How will you measure success?

Plan your work.
Work your plan.

Build Momentum / Think of momentum as the jet fuel that takes your impact and visibility to the next level. Start a wildfire! What can you do to capture the imagination of your market?

Raise the bar.
Exceed expectations.

5) Set aside twenty pages to work on the second habit. Use the first page of this habit as the title page. Write, "Make Rain: Habit #2 - Continually Build Or Create." Add graphics and visuals if that's your thing.

6) How can you get better at continually building or creating? Make it real. Be specific. Develop a new habit. As a reminder, Rome was not built in a day. Be gentle with yourself. Progress, not perfection.

7) Celebrate! It's not easy to do this kind of work, but it is worthwhile. You are investing in yourself! You are

learning to own your Black Sheep voice and powers. Do something nice for yourself. Get in the habit of celebrating your victories, large and small.

One person's normal may be your version of grand. It's relative to the situation at hand. Where are you in your story? What chapter are you about to write? Get clear. Press forward. Work your plan. Climb the mountain. Plant your flag. Big things happen when you dig deep.

Make rain!

CHAPTER #8

OUR SACRED WALK

Your story matters. Each step you take. Steps that await. Inner battles won. Demons that remain. Good habits to keep you sane. Your truth. Filter-free. Order up! One Black Sheep being! As an aside, take pride in the story born from your life. Lessons learned. Bridges burned. Time spent with loved ones. Milestones achieved. Wisdom gained. Impact unique to you alone. Your value is unmistakable.

The path is life. Walking that path is a reverent act. Each minute matters. The daily dance has a rhythm. An ebb and flow. The music of meaningful existence is found in moments. Tender moments. Brave moments. Our souls stir. The right things get done. What does it all mean? A poignant question for the rest stops along the way. Easy answers do not exist! We find ourselves in the gray.

Our walk is a sacred walk. It's the journey we begin from our first breath until the end. How to find your way? Patiently proceed. How to come into your own? Patiently proceed. How to double down on the impact you crave? Patiently proceed. Live an authentic life. Avoid the hype. Stand on solid ground. Life unfolds one chapter at a time. Exist within your story! Grab a pen. Write the narrative.

SURRENDER

Drop the armor. Be fully present. Submit to the situation or task at hand. Anything less feels off. Less satisfying. Untrue. Showing up is the only option. Ugh. I have nothing left to give! Go away! Keeping the door open takes work. It's vital work.

I bought my mom a stuffed teddy bear when she battled cancer. It has been with me since her passing over thirty years ago. My therapist recommended keeping it close as I wrapped up this book. Feel the feels, Bobby Ford! As I pondered writing this chapter, a tsunami of emotion hit from every angle. Raise the bridge! Lower the gate! It was a lot to process. I pulled my mom's teddy bear close. It worked. Tears poured out of me like a broken water main. I have given so much to this rebel tome.

Why pay such a high price?

Our world needs more Black Sheep! When courageous thinkers and creators push the envelope, they transform society in breathtaking, pivotal ways. Hoist the Black Sheep flag, me hearties! When our kind unapologetically raises hell for the right reasons, we elevate the human experience. Even so, it takes a toll. Outliers carry a heavy load few see or understand. Not all of us. To each their own. Still, in my experience, even the most confident rebels face moments of intense doubt, depression, or anxiety. Mental health matters. How to find our way without surrendering the armor that keeps us stuck?

ESSAY #1: FIND THE ART

Pounding on the keyboard like a brain-dead zombie does not make for good writing. Spicing up turns of phrase because, well, why not? Everything is better with hot sauce! Also, not a stellar approach. Fuck me! My eyes roll into the back of my head.

Are you here with me, Bobby?
Are you fully present?

One mantra got me back on the page when my writing was pregnant with potential but lacked a pulse. Find the art! Find the art in the story, moments, and nuances. Find the art in my confessions and realizations, the shared pain offered as an endless refrain. Insight with an edge. Jump off the ledge. Find the art!

Another 100 foot wave.
Stay in the water.
Surrender to the moment.

The mantra became my chisel when crafting this book. Just so you know, I fought it every step of the way. Kicking off a writing session was like trying to calm a screaming two-year-old on fifty pounds of sugar! Eventually, I got to a place of surrender. When I did, the world disappeared. All that remained was a transparent, fully present human being. Anything less would have neutered this book.

ESSAY #2: HAMILTON

After listening to countless hours of the musical *Hamilton*, I sent an urgent email to myself. Only the subject line had words. "Don't end up like Alexander Hamilton!" Let's be honest. I am far from a Founding Father. Still, the degree to which AH pushed himself, the trauma that fueled his unrelenting drive, and the price he paid each step of the way. It struck a raw nerve.

In the opening song, *Alexander Hamilton*, we hear the tale of a man who had every reason to quit with few to survive. Rather than perish, Alexander focused on the things he had yet to do, followed by the lyrics "just you wait, just you wait." It brought back my mid-twenties as though they were yesterday. Give me a chance! I'll rise above my circumstance! I had much to prove.

Emancipation. Red Ford Tempo University. The pink gorilla. Two short films and a play. Improv. My business career. This book. What's behind the next door? Less work. More fun. I'm guessing the last two landed in this tome after my Hamilton email! As of this writing, I have listened to the first song sixty-seven times. To what end? Have I lost my mind? The songs from Hamilton helped me surrender to the art, structure, and cadence necessary to craft this rebel tome. Stiff? Lighten up! In control? Let go!

The tools always exist.
Find your tools.

Seventeen songs into the Hamilton soundtrack is the heartfelt piece *That Would Be Enough*. It is a tender, beautifully played exchange between a husband and wife. Alexander is racked with self-doubt. His sense of worth has bottomed out, only to discover his wife, Eliza, is expecting. "Look around, look around," she repeats. Everything that matters already exists. Take stock. Live in the now. It's a hard truth to trust, is it not? In the last three lines, we find a core tenet of this book.

> *"And I could be enough*
> *And we could be enough*
> *That would be enough"*

Art matters. Even more so when we let it into our hearts. How to chart our course without seeing with all of our senses? Now more than ever, bringing down our walls is no easy feat. The level of chaos in the world is beyond any I've known in almost sixty years of existence. All the same, do we really have a choice? In the safety of darkness is the absence of light.

ESSAY #4: IN THE MIRROR

How to surrender? It has nothing to do with giving up. It has everything to do with letting go of our armor, assumptions, expectations, bad habits, anything, really, that stands in the way of progress. How to heal the pain we pretend does not exist? How to do our thing if we refuse to get out of the way? It's a learning process, in my view. Trusting ourselves. Seeing the good despite our flaws. Coping. Developing healthier habits. Meaningful connection. Being present. The more I let go, the more I get to know myself. It's an important shift to embrace.

We all yearn. We all crave. It's the stuff we never say. What will people think? Worries in our brains. The hands of time turn. Silent, no more! We speak our peace. Our truth is released. The person in the mirror, more clear. More dear. More treasured. We come alive, no longer willing to hide. We find freedom when our humanity is on full display.

Pretending to have our shit together (no one does) pays homage to false gods that exploit our self-doubt. We find peace, in my view, by getting comfortable in our own skin. The prerequisite to owning my value is accepting my imperfections. That will never change! It took forty years to start getting comfortable in my own skin. My suggestion? Start earlier. The peace we seek can only be found in the mirror, my friend.

Deep, right? Let's go a little deeper! Yes, Black Sheep are different, but to what degree? This is not a one size fits all lifestyle. We have to carve our own path. My version of the Black Sheep life could be vastly different than your version. It's an intimate, vulnerable *pilgrimage* we go on throughout our lives. Surrender to the pilgrimage. Stay curious. Be a seeker. Remain a student.

TRUST

Believing despite the evidence is crucial. We explore the unknown. Blaze a trail. Take huge risks. We keep at it even when loved ones tell us to quit. It's not impulsive. Trusting our talent and the passions we pursue is an act of faith. What inspires that faith? The answer may prove elusive, even confusing. It's not a calculation you can work out on paper. And yet, instinctively, it makes total sense. If nothing else, we are a contradiction. Being different embraces a bit of chaos. I love that part! It is a necessary ingredient to charting our own course.

Embrace the unknowable.
Surf your instincts.

Do you trust your ability to weather the storm? Do you trust your aspirations? Do you trust your value? It's a sacred pact we make with ourselves. Absent self-trust, Black Sheep struggle. Still, it takes time to trust our path. As we navigate life, we find our voice and plant our flag. It sounds momentous, but that is rarely the case. In the real world, we come into our own over many years. It's a polishing process. The purpose of this book is to lend a hand as that process unfolds.

Trusting myself was put to the test when writing this book. Repeatedly, this rebel tome demanded more of me than I ever thought possible to give. While steadfast in my resolve, I struggled with intense overwhelm and self-doubt. What the hell am I doing? The writing required emotional availability well beyond anything I had ever experienced. To pay such a price required a compelling purpose. At times, that purpose was clear. Other times, not so much. The experience of coming into our own never ends. It becomes about different things as the years' pass, but the journey remains. To get this book done, I had to trust that this rebel tome would substantially impact people's lives. That was the standard. Anything less was not an option.

ESSAY #1: ART IMITATES LIFE

Paul Newman. Joanne Woodward. Hollywood legends. Countless awards. Six children, three of them from Newman's first marriage. Charitable donations in the millions. It makes sense Newman would commission a peer to interview friends, family, people from the film industry, and Newman himself for a memoir the actor planned to write. Ten years before his death, Newman burned the taped interviews around the same time he torched a tuxedo. Theories flourish as to his reasons.

Lucky for us, transcripts were made of those audio tapes, which became the basis for Ethan Hawk's superb HBO documentary, *The Last Movie Stars*. Hawke's intimate approach plays more like a group of friends exploring human nature than it does a fan film. It struck a chord.

Notable is how ordinary Newman and Woodward felt regarding their struggles. They lived extraordinary lives as messy, complex beings. It's a gripping tale.

Early in the series, Paul Newman shares (via George Clooney's voice acting from a transcript) his envy for the bohemians of his era, like Martin Scorsese, Marlon Brando, and Jack Nicholson. Newman's observation that his eccentric contemporaries were not trying to "become something they aren't" sparked a realization. The choice to be yourself is a choice to trust yourself. They are one and the same. Anyone, Black Sheep or otherwise, benefits from such a decision. How else to live a life that is true to who we are as human beings?

Later in the documentary, I discovered Elia Kazan. The director's list of accomplishments boggles the mind. When did the man sleep? Among Kazan's notable works is a poem he wrote for the thespians of his time. While the full version is a gem, I found magic specific to this book in the last three lines. In simplicity, we find truth. I offer the last three lines of Elia Kazan's Actors Vow.

> *"I will work on it.*
> *I will raise my voice.*
> *I will be heard."*

In the face of my wrongs, serious mistakes, deep regrets, and more flaws than I can name, nonetheless, I remain. Big ideas. Small ideas. Passion projects that refuse to go away. A voice with things to say! I choose to trust myself.

ESSAY #2: RADICAL FAITH

I view you as someone worth seeing. Can I walk with you? Will you walk with me? We have much work to do! Suffering. Oppression. Exquisite ideas that are hungry to take flight. Passion projects. A type of capitalism that makes the world a better place. It's time for a revolution! Not born from violence or rage. Stable soil seeds lasting change. Welcome to the neighborhood!

In the *Six Principles Of Nonviolence*, Dr. Martin Luther King Jr. writes, "Nonviolence believes the universe is on the side of justice." Trust writ large is an act of faith. My history with organized religion has been, for the most part, negative. Groupthink anointed by God Almighty is not my jam. Nor do I play nice to get a given group's blessings. Big shocker! And yet, I have long been a man of deep faith.

My spirituality is rooted in the steadfast belief that a power greater than myself operates behind the scenes.

Heaven. Hell. Reincarnation. Who knows? I certainly don't have a clue! Regardless, I live from a place of purpose. Our existence is the miracle.

Purity tests are a lie.
Don't drink the Kool-aid!

If humanism, Buddhism, The Force, and 12 Step had a four-way that resulted in a baby, that would be my faith tradition. Seriously? A group sex metaphor when talking about spirituality! Lebowski and Skywalker are clanking glasses and toasting my name in another world. Dude, you do not know the power of white Russians! Cue the close-up shot of a clenched fist in a black glove.

Cheers, fellas!

When my mom passed over three decades ago, I chose to do her eulogy. On one side of my mother's casket stood a minister. Standing on the opposite side, I read from the Bible, 1 Corinthians 13. My mother, despite her flaws, was in heaven. That was the case I was prosecuting. As proof, I cited my mother's never-ending kindness to people from all walks of life. In my final argument, I reread the last sentence from the biblical verse, "But the greatest of these is love." People wept. I choked up. It was a stout yet tender tribute. The prosecution rests.

The minister, who stood well over six feet tall, leaned into his microphone. Extending his arms like he was reenacting the crucifixion, he asked if I had been called to do God's work? Taken off guard, I paused for a few beats, then leaned into my microphone. "Was it a collect call?" I responded. "If so, I don't think I accepted the charges!" My relationship with God has been tenuous at best.

And yet, I would be dead without my faith in a power greater than myself. I'm sorry, but there is no way to soften that statement. Too many miracles have graced my life to not think otherwise. Do I believe God saved my life? No, I do not. But I have always sensed a presence greater than myself bumping about in my life. At times, the feeling is faint. Other times, it's front and center. No matter, my earthly existence *serves a sacred purpose*. Whether that's bullshit or not does not matter. I trust that my walk through life is sacred. It keeps me accountable. It shores up my resilience. In trust, I find meaning.

Words to the wise, making yourself the higher power never ends well. Humans are talented at a great many things. Historically speaking, playing God is not one of those things. Connect to the sacred part of your earthly existence. What might that look like?

WALK

Our trek began with a note whose final line read, "Dare to open the doors that make you tremble." Absent such courage, we fade away. Little to say. Day after day. Night after night. Falling in line. Waiting in line. How the hell did I get stuck in line?

Art ignored. Activism stored. Rights retracted. Social enterprise shoved in a box. The status quo turns the key to the lock. Click-pop! Then ever so casually, business as usual throws the key away.

Fuck that noise!
It's time to go loud.

The world's gone mad. Time to do your thing! Raise some hell. Ease the pain. Find solutions. End tyranny. Sow the seeds of change. Art to create. Ideas to build. Rights to reclaim. Let's put an end to the insane!

We are the revolution.
#BlackSheepProud

ESSAY #1: BEYOND THE BARRICADE

I first bumped into the affable Igor Novikov when he appeared on the MSNBC show, Deadline: White House.

As a savvy former advisor to President Zelensky, I expected Igor to rock stiff responses and power suits. Instead, he comes off as the Comic-Con dad who regularly drags his family to Disneyland. When Novikov does TV interviews, he's usually wearing a graphic tee shirt, often with a stuffed Baby Yoda in the background.

The stories he tells cut through the fog of war. No fluff. No pretense. It's as if Mr. Rodgers became a war correspondent. I respond to his Instagram posts often, offering feeble words of encouragement. Perhaps, in some small way, they help. Igor's searing commentary on the unjust invasion of Ukraine hits home because it's relatable.

Daria Kolomiec, an artist in Ukraine and New York, is a force of nature! On any given day, her Instagram might feature stories about wine, air raid sirens, food, Ukrainian soldiers, and video of her spinning records as a celebrated DJ. If Willy Wonka made energy drinks, one of them would be named after Daria!

While taking acting classes in New York City in 2022, she marched in a Pride parade, advocated for her homeland, and still found time to make music. How is this possible? When her studies concluded, it was back to Ukraine to fight for freedom, then back to the United States. Like Igor, she brings the brutality of the war to your living room as though you have known her your entire life. Kolomiec's magic is her transparency.

Two extraordinary ordinary beings.
Slava Ukraini!

One day, I will visit Ukraine, so I can shove my hands into the soil of Bucha. Germans, Brits, Italians, Japanese and others need to do the same because buried in that soil is the cost of freedom. Skip the press op. Just stick your hands in the dirt, and close your eyes. Ponder the price. Honor the sacrifice.

Walking your path requires claiming ground beyond the barricade. War. Oppression. Poverty. Hate. Rights once held that are now denied. Impossible odds. An over-the-top idea that's stuck. Improbable projects. Art waiting in the wings. Whatever the barricade, you have to get beyond it and stake your claim.

ESSAY #2: INTO THE LIGHT

A six-figure income when young and still, I felt empty inside. My visibility and impact soared. The job titles got sexier. And while I certainly took pride in how far I had come, like a drug, it was all about the next high. How could I push even harder? I'm never satisfied.

During my first year in AA, my peers talked me into volunteering at a local homeless shelter on Thanksgiving. Truth be told, I had never been so terrified in my life! Safety was not the issue. My business persona would be of little use at a homeless shelter. There was no place to hide! The guy that ran the center sized me up in an instant. He assigned me coffee duty. My job was simple. Wander the crowd, asking homeless people if they wanted a cup of coffee? If they did, I got their coffee and spent time with them. Jumping out of an airplane without a parachute would have been easier.

As I catatonically wandered the dystopian world that had me in its grip, I noticed a young man, early twenties, short, frantically pacing back and forth. Strapped onto his slight frame was a monstrous backpack. It looked like a Hobbit had somehow stuffed a troll into their knapsack to make a point. What that point might be, I had not a clue! As I approached the young Troll carrying lad, his hands began to tremble. With some gentle coaxing, I got him to sit with me at a nearby table.

Danny was his name. He confessed to severe learning disabilities, which is why his parents abandoned him on the side of the road when he was a young boy. Who does that to a child? His sister checked on him now and then, but that was about it. After a few minutes of small talk, Danny suddenly grabbed my hands. He wanted me to pray with him. Before I could respond, he started emptying his backpack. It was mainly filled with books, a portable version of Red Ford Tempo University. One of them was a Bible. It was time to pray. I will never forget Danny or our time together.

Our group went to an AA meeting as soon as we left the homeless shelter. In sharing the story, I couldn't stop crying. Finally, thanks to Danny, the dam broke. My days as a zombie ended when I stopped pretending. When the door appeared, it made me tremble. No matter, it was time to serve coffee to a young man with a bag full of books. Who knows what's on the other side of the door? There is only one way to find out.

When do you feel like a zombie? When do you fully present and, therefore, fully alive? Daria, the Ukrainian I wrote about a moment ago, did a post today about her incredible life. She shared that sentiment from a war zone. How we choose to walk determines everything.

If you are young, learn from my mistakes. If not, there is no time like the present. Make a conscious choice to be a fully present and engaged human being. We find freedom when our beauty walks with our beast in the light of day. Choose freedom.

ESSAY #3: JUST TO WALK

Hands to clay. Clutching. Shaping. Adding. Removing. An orchestra of instinct plays Beethoven's 5th through her fingertips. For months on end, she sculpts. A Maestro of nuance driven by an image painted on her soul. Gradually, her heart-infused vision is given life. Three delightful children at play. Pure joy is beautifully cast in bronze. It's palpable. Such is the stunning work of Living Master Angela Mia De la Vega-Goga.

Remodeling homes, she dances alone, often in high tops. In claiming space, she puts a face on soulful self-care. Health food or junk food? Solitary or full-on loud? She's stylish DIY covered in paint. Lots of paint! Dope-ass insights on authenticity. Encouragement to slow down. You'll find her cornucopia of content on all the major platforms. Actor. Dancer. Bass player? Entrepreneur. Such is the eclectic world of Megan Batoon.

Why did you buy this book? What were you hoping to find? Rewind the story. Go back in time. Close your eyes. What do you crave as you turn the page?

Travel True North.
Do your thing.

The Parkland shooting in 2018 took seventeen cherished lives. Rise up! A small group of teen survivors raises their voices. The clarity of their message rips through the rhetoric. Political leaders with blood on their hands come into view. Rise up! Millions take to the streets to protest against gun violence. The activist organization March For Our Lives is born.

Traditional Italian food reimagined. The aroma of culinary revolution wafts through the air. Artisan food. Handcrafted. Each bite is a gift of sensations. Each bite speaks to the moment. Reverence is always on the menu!. An imagination that knows no bounds. Ideas invade left and right, even when a plate violently crashes to the ground. Such is the magic of Maestro Chef Massimo Bottura.

Our tribe is magnificent in its diversity! Hippies. Healers. Social change dealers. Artists. Activists. Storytellers with things to say. What fills the void as you turn the page?

Our humanity is why our walk is sacred. We are a hot mess of beautifully brilliant with a side of being different. And, perhaps, our own brand of vanilla. Shhh! Don't tell anyone! However you might describe yourself, it's your journey to walk. The broken parts and the remarkable parts are of equal value. Pristine is a noxious illusion that only leads to heartache. Imperfections. Rough edges. Oh, hell yeah! It's your adventure. What rocks your world?

Write a book! What in the hell was I thinking? It was a task. The next step. The Universe knew different. My therapist knew better. Me? Not so much. Paul Riser fans? While I don't have kids to carry on my new name, I have my experience, strength, and hope, gifted to this rebel tome. Words of wisdom born from trauma. Tools to beat the odds acquired while navigating life. The inspiration to be yourself born from a lifetime of being Black Sheep Proud™. Etched on the page are my greatest hits and worst oversights. Together, we walk.

It feels weird, slightly surreal, to be writing the final paragraph. Had I not written this book, we never would have met. Our time together never would have happened. One decision can alter the impact you leave behind. Dare to open the doors that make you tremble!

I get the ghosts and understand the pain. All the crap rattling around in your brain. But in the grand scheme of things, you're the solution. Find your way. Do your thing. Have the impact you crave.

ABOUT THE AUTHOR

Art with an edge! Jump off the ledge! Breaking down walls to get people to think is my jam. It's never about the medium. It's always about the work and the broader purpose that work serves. Forty years of writing. Two short films. One improvised play. And, ya know, I wrote this book. In another life, I pushed the envelope in the ad game, management consulting, and creative direction. Swearing is fun. Street tacos are heaven. Geekery is bliss. Aspiring beach bum, hopefully in Hawaii.

bobbyford.io / Workshops - Merch - Consulting - Projects
@bobbyford_io / Instagram

Interior Artwork / Art Fuentes
arftheartiste.com